The Wandering Hinjew

a memoir

Robert Sherman, Ph.D.

Wandering in the Words Press

Wandering in the Words Press:
2131 Burns St, Nashville, Tennessee 37216
www.wanderinginthewordspress.com

This is a memoir and contains autobiographical elements about the
author. The author has made every attempt to recreate events, locales and
conversations from his memories of them. In order to maintain their
anonymity, the author may have changed or may have left out the names
of individuals, places and identifying characteristics and details such as
physical properties, occupations and places of residence.

This book is not intended as a substitute for therapy. The reader should
consult with a licensed psychotherapist in matters relating to his/her
mental health.

PUBLISHED BY WANDERING IN THE WORDS PRESS

WANDERING
IN THE WORDS

ISBN-10: 0990919366
ISBN-13: 978-0-9909193-6-0
First Edition

DEDICATION

This book is dedicated to my two gloriously beautiful sons who have probably taught me as much as I have taught them. I hope that something that follows will allow each of you to better understand the environmental soup into which you were hatched. I wish for you both to deeply and fully experience yourselves as loveable and worthy, and that you know how much your parents love you. I do realize that I have not always contributed to that reality. I will continue to do my best to help you knock out whatever dents remain.

The mark of successful parenting is to raise kids who can afford their own therapy.

The photograph reflects a moment that is happening out in the world, and also one that is happening in the minds of the photographer and the viewer.
The fact that the moment is fleeting and will never get repeated adds to its appeal. A photograph acknowledges this transience. The best ones attach meaning to it.

—David Butow, "Seeing Buddha: A Photographic Journey"

An artist is he who can balance strong contrasts, who can combine opposing forms and forces in significant unity.

—Jean Toomer, *Essentials*

TABLE OF CONTENTS

INTRODUCTION

Imagine driving in your new car on a wide-open highway. No one is in front of you to impede your progress. Three hundred horses surge at your beck and call with just the slightest calf flex. What a glorious experience! As master of your magnificent universe, you can go anywhere at any time. The comforting interior temperature is matched by the reverberation of your favorite music echoing from the eight speakers equalized just the way you like them at a volume that invites your cells to dance with abandon. The cup of coffee that stands at attention a few inches away not only adds a friendly aroma, it also supplies the nurturance that exquisitely completes this most perfect moment of human existence.

Then in an instant and without warning, another and much larger car slams into the passenger door. You hear the horrible explosion of shattering glass and the alien scream of metal twisting and tearing beyond its capacity. You feel indescribable pain. Terror and shock grip you as you realize your total inability to control in any way what will happen next. You don't even know if you will survive.

How quickly the omnipotence turns to abject powerlessness. Just when it couldn't get any worse, you realize that the driver of the other car was one of your parents; this was no accident!

Welcome to the world of childhood sexual abuse. What I have just described is not a function of any added violence. This is what it feels like under the "best of circumstances."

I know this firsthand because at age forty-six I learned that I had been sexually abused when I was a very young child. Prior to middle age, I had no conscious awareness of the abuse. Regardless of the lack of awareness, the abuse shaped every aspect of my existence. In retrospect, I needed all of this time to gain the conscious awareness of what had happened. Once I had, my perspective on my entire life changed dramatically.

A perspective is a viewpoint, an attitude, a way of looking at the world. Usually we don't question our fundamental perspectives, or we question them only enough to confirm their solidity. They form the bedrock of our worldviews, and they *must* be true because they emerged organically from the experience of direct perception. Right? What could be more fundamentally unquestionable?

Most of us imagine our perceptions to be objective—that we see and hear things as they are. This is one of our greatest acts of self-deception because it is far from the truth. Emotions shape perception. Experiences shape perception.

Environment and economic factors shape perception. Even the language we learn as children influences how we think and what we allow ourselves to see. Or not see.

I am a psychologist, and to illustrate the subjective aspect of perception for my clients I hold up a white Styrofoam cup and ask them what shape the top of the cup is. I deliberately hold the cup at a slight angle. Only artists give the correct answer: "ellipse." Everyone else says "circle" because they know the shape from prior experience. The reality, however, is that the pattern of light on their retinas is only circular when the cup is perpendicular to their field of vision. I then ask them what color the cup is. Again, only the artists will say "gray." Everyone else says "white," because they know the cup to be white from prior experience. The color is only white when the illumination is approximately 5,500 Kelvin. Such is the subtle power of unexamined perspective.

In this book, I will share with you how my perspectives of my worth, my role, and even my identity were created and how they changed over the course of sixty-eight years. As my perspectives regarding myself changed, how I viewed others and the world around me changed, as well. Because the many wonderful, terrible, heartbreaking, and heart-opening things I saw along the way were of vital importance, I will include some of my photographs to provide you a clearer visual image.

The world of childhood sexual abuse does not come with an instruction manual or map. It is a world of silence and secrets. In this world, those who are in charge act as if everything is normal. There is no victim, because nothing ever happened. Every young child views his or her parents as gods, and it is crystal clear to the child that God never makes a mistake. Therefore, the child believes he got what he deserved.

Individuals who have been in car accidents often experience symptoms of post-traumatic stress disorder. Things that had no emotional charge before the accident can become potential sources of significant anxiety. Such symptoms might include panicking at the sight of brake lights, fearing intersections, or hyperventilating at the thought of driving altogether. For a sexual abuse survivor, post-traumatic stress disorder symptoms might include reacting negatively to the smell of alcohol, dodging alone time with anyone of the opposite sex, wearing clothing that hides the body, trying hard to go unnoticed, or feeling guilty when sexually aroused. This list is far from exhaustive.

The abused child often feels both trapped and powerless. Such feelings lead to the mindset of, *If I don't move, maybe I won't be noticed.* The child may unconsciously learn how to anesthetize herself so that devastating feelings won't overwhelm her. This anesthesia does not go away with adulthood.

Any competent mechanic will tell you that once the frame gets bent, the car is irreparably damaged. You can knock out the dents and even put on a fresh coat of paint, but the reality *for a car* is that those changes will be cosmetic at best. For the vast majority of sexual abuse survivors, their belief is that the damage has been done, and they cannot ever be repaired.

Consciously or not, this "truth" of irreparable damage becomes the perspective upon which the child builds the rest of his or her life. The terror of total vulnerability in a war zone becomes a potential component in every subsequent relationship or interaction.

There is a controversy in the therapeutic community about the creation of false memories and whether it is even possible to repress such an event as sexual abuse. In my case, I had no conscious awareness of the possibility of sexual abuse in my life until I was forty-six. Yes, it is possible to create false memories, but this fact is irrelevant to my present concerns. In my own journey, I have focused on discovering my final answer to the question as to whether or not I am irreparably damaged. I am committed to rooting out any remaining ways that I remain in hiding. As a psychologist, I do not view therapy as a prosecution. My endeavor is to help my clients answer the very same question for themselves. Whether or not the perpetrator in question is ever "convicted as charged" is irrelevant to the success of the therapy. What is relevant in my clients' therapy is whether or not they can learn how to leave the war zone. It is also highly relevant whether or not they can summon the courage to look deeply into themselves and see and experience who they really are.

The child has no choice but to accept as truth what his parents have told him. The child has no choice but to learn his worth as a function of what he experiences and how he is treated. As an adult, a person must summon a tremendous amount of courage and strength to risk re-examining "the facts" that have for so long been experienced as gospel.

This book details my own journey out of that war zone. My impetus for writing this memoir is a result of trying to answer two questions that, on the surface, appear to be light years away from sexual abuse. First, "Why do I take photographs?" And second, "Why was it so easy to think of myself as an artist as a therapist but so difficult to also think of myself as an artist whose medium is photography?" My hope is that by the end of this memoir the relevance will be obvious and that, as a reader, you will have learned something of value along the way.

In the pages that follow, I will attempt to take you around the world in my photography and at the same time take you around my inner world. I believe that seeing the beauty in others allows us to glimpse that same beauty in ourselves. I will attempt to share what I was aware of at different stages of my life, how it influenced who I thought I was, and what I did as a result.

Along the way, my spiritual beliefs became an essential part of my existence and recovery. I do not really believe in heaven, but I find the concept useful for many of my clients. Here is how I make use of the concept of heaven: After we die, we do indeed find ourselves in front of the pearly gates. But there is no book and no Saint Peter. Instead we find ourselves stark naked standing in front of a full-size, absolutely perfect mirror. Our arrival actuates a neon sign that reads as follows:

Welcome to Heaven. We have only one question for you to answer. Your answer will determine whether or not you will be allowed entrance this time around. Please be certain to answer with perfect honesty. We will abide by your response. Please do not attempt to deceive us in any way. We know your truth. Do you believe that you are worthy of entering heaven?

Those who answer "Yes" and do not hear a chorus of laughter in their heads or feel a surge of doubt or terror, find the gates opening wide. The rest of us, who are still behaving like Phil Connors in the movie *Groundhog Day*, have to return for another life. We have to learn to see the truth of who we really are so that we can stand naked before God (and even our spouses) and not be mortified about the toxic waste at the core of our being.

I earned a doctorate from New York University in 1974, and I have been a therapist since 1977. The most useful concept for me in helping the vast majority of my clients has been to assist them to get in touch with their shame. As their therapist, my intention is to provide them with an environment that is safe enough for them to risk sharing that shame with me so that they can see it through their own adult eyes. Not surprisingly, I would characterize my own journey as exactly the same.

I frequently give my clients an article written by Phoebe Phelps entitled "Remembering as the Task of Therapy." In this article, she cites Alice Miller as stating that, "...what was so enabling for Jesus Christ was not that He was the Son of God, but that his parents *knew* He was the Son of God." It is Phelps' contention that therapy ought to be about getting back in touch with our own divinity. Perhaps we continue to be reincarnated until we can look in that mirror and hear a very clear "yes" and nothing else.

***

About the photography: I've made every effort to reproduce as faithfully as possible the thirty-three images that are an integral part of my memoir. However, printing costs and paper quality make it impossible to render the exact color quality. Please visit my website's "Wandering Hinjew" album for a more complete experience of the photography: www.bobshermanphotography.com.

CHAPTER ONE
Public Suicide

During the winter of 2010, I was having lunch with Roy Hutton, one of Nashville's leading therapists. Roy asked me to give a talk at NPI (Nashville Psychotherapy Institute, a group for psychotherapists) about my approach to therapy and what I think it's all about. My response was to laugh. "Why are you interested in watching my public suicide?" I asked.

***

I grew up in Queens, New York. I have been lucky enough to have lived in a number of foreign countries and to have traveled to many different places all over the world. I am not good at learning foreign languages; in school I was remarkably consistent in my ability to earn a D in French for seven years in a row. Thankfully, up until November 2007, I had an unbroken string of attempting to communicate in French in foreign lands and being responded to in English. That string was broken in Kampot, Cambodia, when the man who was talking to me in French didn't know English. I learned enough Farsi to be able to get around in Iran and Afghanistan. I have been able to adapt fairly well to being an outsider in these places.

So when I moved in 2005 from Toms River, New Jersey, to Nashville, Tennessee, in order to be with my fiancée, I was confident that I'd be able to make the transition. Up until that time, I had been fortunate in my professional life. I had been in private practice as a psychologist for more than twenty-three years. In the second week after opening my first private practice, I had a waiting list of potential clients. Prior to opening that practice, I had been the Chief Psychologist at a large community mental health center, so I was well known in the area. None of this prepared me for my experience moving to Nashville.

I now live in an area where one's answer to the following question is of vital importance: *What church do you belong to?* In my preceding fifty-nine years, no one had ever asked me that question. My spiritual life is at the core of my existence, but I don't own stock in any religious corporation. My belief is that all paths are valid, and they all lead to the same place. I'm attracted to any endeavor that will allow people to feel a deep sense of connection to something larger than themselves and allow them to realize that, in reality, religion isn't about "us" versus "them." I'm in favor of any endeavor that will allow a person to change his or her perspective so that he or she can feel worthy and loveable and to also experience a deep sense of contentment. Unfortunately, that is not what I experience in many of the houses of worship in Nashville.

The area in which I'm living is the wealthiest conservative Republican community in the country. My fiancée and I didn't know this when we purchased our house. We had been looking for a house for quite a while, and this was the first one we'd seen that we both liked, so we grabbed it. We now live in a home at which the sign I had placed on our front lawn supporting Barack Obama in 2008 was destroyed three times. Just last week I wished someone a "Happy Martin Luther King Day." His response was, "Happy James Earl Ray Day."

I say all of this to describe what began in 2005 as a journey to regain my center. My move to Nashville brought a number of unexpected but highly significant consequences. I was well aware of the leap I was taking by giving up my wonderfully successful psychotherapy practice. I rationalized that all I would need to do was meet a few people who were in a position to make referrals and I'd be on my way. My previous experience was that, since I was both competent and fluent in *doctorspeak*, I would be able to ask a physician to make one or two "guinea pig" referrals to demonstrate how good I really was. After the test cases reported back that they liked me, the dike would open for many more referrals. Unfortunately, the process doesn't seem to work that way here, and I must admit that I still haven't discovered the magic handshake. When I opened my practice in Nashville, I was confronted with the reality that, at age sixty-one, I was going to have to market myself. I never had to do that when I first went into private practice, because I was already well known as a result of being a chief psychologist. I'm not complaining. At this point—now nine years later—I have a long waiting list.

I also grew quite ill when I moved here, and I wasn't strong enough to work for a year and a half. My fiancée was incredibly wonderful about that, and she let me know that I would have no financial worries until I got back on my feet. She also strongly encouraged me to consider pursuing photography as a full-time career. I was quick to reject that idea for two reasons: I really loved being a part of a therapeutic process, and I believed I wasn't good enough as a photographer.

Another dynamic in the unexpected consequence category was that, early in our relationship, my fiancée started calling me Res instead of Bob. When I started meeting her friends, they also called me Res. The reason the name change occurred was that when she and I would exchange emails, she would sign her emails "BNC" (her initials). After I saw Bob for the second time at the end of my own email, I decided that anyone could be a Bob, so I started signing my emails "RES" (my initials). My girlfriend really liked this because she had too many other Bobs in her life, so this differentiated me. Without realizing it, I had instituted a fundamental shift in perspective: I had changed my name, and I had done so at a moment in which my self worth as a photographer was struggling to be born.

I felt lost after about a year of living in Nashville. I found myself not fitting in spiritually, politically, financially, physically or emotionally. I started to resent being called Res, because rather than recognizing my new name as a potentially powerful shift in perspective, I experienced it as a clear sign of the loss of my identity. I also did not fit in socially. As a New Yorker, I am accustomed to saying things directly. That's not how it's done in these parts.

All of these factors led me to feel like a duck in a desert. Ever since the age of eleven, I had been able to take care of my financial needs, and suddenly I was running a deficit. I was in poor physical condition because I had been dealing with the effects of undiagnosed sleep apnea. That got me in touch with a sense of vulnerability. In so many ways, I felt like I was in a foreign country without a GPS. Psychologically and emotionally, I was in a perfect environment to become aware of the residual effects from my childhood experiences.

I do know that, in my life, the darkest and most painful times have frequently been the Petri dish from which something spiritually magical has grown. When I am in the midst of these difficult times, I am not always marinating in the glory of my gratitude. But frequently, after the dust has settled and my perspective has shifted, I do become aware of the gift that was buried in the pain. I also know that, in my thirty-four years of practice, I have never had a prospective client call me for an appointment because he had heard that I was an interesting guy with whom to talk. A person calls me after his shit has hit the fan and he's afraid that his face will be next.

At this point, some of you might be wondering, "Where is God in all of this?" Obviously, people have widely differing views on whether or not God intervenes in our lives. From my perspective, such interventions would do more harm than good. People generally don't change and grow just because it's a good idea. For most of us, it takes an overwhelming amount of pain and desperation to force us to change, despite the inertia our fear can cause. Such divine interventions would be like helping a butterfly by cutting a hole in its cocoon so that it would not have to struggle to get out. It certainly would save the butterfly a lot of initial pain, but the consequence of that "gift" would be to produce a butterfly that can't fly. Rather than intervention, the more loving approach would be for God to allow us to learn in the only manner that really works.

On a positive note, living in Nashville has allowed me to meet some wonderful people who otherwise would not have been in my life. I enjoy working with my clients, and I have had wonderful opportunities to grow as an artist as a result of relocating here.

Over the years, I have come to realize that the capacities that one develops to survive in an abusive environment have both positive and negative consequences. The task in recovery is to learn what those capacities are and to determine under which circumstances they no longer serve us.

***

During my lunch discussion with Roy, I asked him why anybody else would be interested in my story. His response was that, if they didn't know me, they probably wouldn't be interested enough to learn about me. But they might be interested if it allowed them to better understand their own stories and if it taught them something of value for their own lives. So this book is what I hope will not be my public suicide.

***

Around 1995 I started sending out holiday cards that I had composed. The theme of each card was not a conscious endeavor on my part. Each theme spontaneously arose out of a repeating theme in either myself or my clients for that year. Starting in 2003, I began to use one of my photographs as the front of the card.

The following was my card for 2011. The photo for this card, "Bye Mommy," is a young girl on a carousel.

***

Fear is rarely a good chauffeur.
The really great stuff is usually beyond
the speed limits imposed by the illusions
of who we think we are.

BYE MOMMY - LONDON, ENGLAND, 11/06

I took this photo in London at Covent Garden. The technique of moving the camera as the photographer takes the shot is called panning. With panning, one focuses on the main subject and then moves the camera to blur the background. When successful, the techniques show a sense of movement.

I have no idea which of my photographs other people will like. This image is especially popular with adult women. Many women start speaking in that high-pitched voice reserved for infants and puppies when they view this shot.

For me, this image symbolizes the instinctive movement towards power and independence. The little girl looks back towards her mother for affirmation and security while at the same time she revels in the energy of her newfound power. Soon she will turn away from that security and face her future.

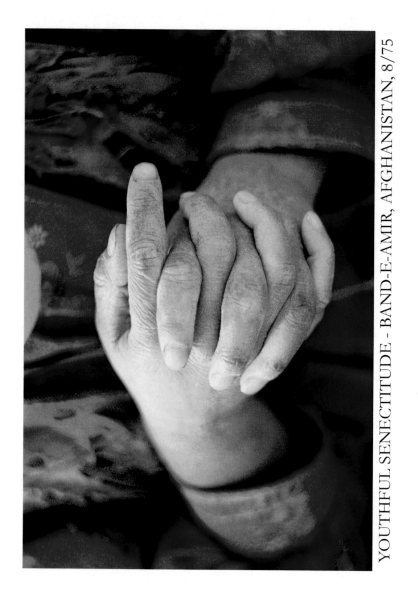

YOUTHFUL SENECTITUDE - BAND-E-AMIR, AFGHANISTAN, 8/75

CHAPTER TWO
A "Chance" Meeting

On July 2, 2010, my then fiancée was about to perform at a benefit concert. The benefit included dinner before the show. The venue had picnic tables in the back, and I was sitting at one of those tables talking to my daughter-in-law. In what was, for me, a most uncharacteristic show of social grace, I leaned over to the other couple sitting at the same table, reached out my hand, and said to the guy, "Hi, I'm Bob Sherman."

"The photographer?" he asked. This was not on my list of expected replies. I asked his name and asked if he was "on The Dose" (to be explained later). He said, "no."

So in my newly learned Southern gentility I asked, "How the hell do you know that I'm a photographer?" This exchange was the beginning of a wonderful but unanticipated chapter in my life.

His name was Anthony, and he was a photographer for *Nashville Arts Magazine*. That very morning, Anthony had stopped in the middle of a photo shoot at the home of Darrell Scott (a wonderful singer/songwriter and parent) when he and the editor had seen one of my photos on Darrell's living room wall. It was my photograph entitled "Youthful Senectitude" that had caught their attention. At that time, that photograph (pictured here at the start of this chapter) had only existed in two places: Darrell's living room and my dining room. What were the chances of Anthony learning of my existence at 10 a.m. and then meeting me at 7 p.m. on the same day?

The evening progressed, and Anthony and I joked while we both took pictures of the concert. Near the end of the meeting, he told me that his editor would contact me to explore the possibility of doing a story about me. When this took place, I had been a Nashville resident for about five years. During those five years, I had learned to not expect people to follow through with what they said they would do. So while the idea of having my photography featured in a magazine was wonderfully exciting, I wasn't yet closing my practice as a clinical psychologist.

Three weeks later, I received a voicemail at my office from someone named Paul who spoke with a marked British accent. Paul identified himself as the editor of the *Nashville Arts Magazine*. He wondered if I would mind meeting him in order to discuss a six- or seven-page article that he would like to do on my work!

Now let's see. Would I mind?

My fingers broke the speed of light dialing his number, and we set up a time for him and one of his writers to come to my office to interview me. Paul Polycarpou was remarkably friendly, and because the phone conversation was going very nicely, I used that opportunity to manifest some of my New York *chutzpah* (Yiddish for a combination of gall and balls) to let him know that the article that I'd love for him to write would be entitled, "The Shrink Who Takes Pictures."

Why not try to get some free advertising for my therapy practice?

Paul told me that that was something close to what he had in mind, so I was shocked, pleased, and very excited. Paul then said that it would be a good idea for us to time the article to coincide with my *next show*. When I finally stopped laughing, I told Paul that I'd love to time the article with my *first show*. Paul seemed quite surprised that I had never had an exhibition of my work.

***

The interview took place in my psychotherapy office. I had been a psychologist in private practice for twenty-eight years by then (twenty-three years in New Jersey and five in Nashville). I had completed my doctorate in 1974 at New York University, and I had been working as a therapist since 1977. I was confident in being able to talk about my artistry and creativity *as a therapist,* but I had yet to perceive myself as an artist-photographer. I had fairly good technical skills, and I had been lucky enough to travel to some fascinating places where I'd photographed cool stuff, but I had no idea how my photographs impacted anyone else.

At that time, my shame significantly influenced my capacity to evaluate the quality of my photography. I had far better clarity about what was wrong with my shots than what was right with them. I could easily talk about what techniques I didn't know rather than what made my work special. I also had a notion that, since the shots I took came so easily, that ease must indicate an absence of art.

The first question that Paul asked me in our interview was, "As a photographer and artist, what is it that you are trying to convey to your viewer at the time you take your shot?"

"I've never thought of this before," I said. "As far as I know, the only person I am trying to please is myself."

The rest of the interview went well. I was so grateful to have the opportunity to think about the questions Paul asked and to be in the presence of an expert who was interested in my thoughts and my photographs.

Paul expected the article to be six or seven pages long and planned to feature about fifteen of my shots. However, I was totally blown away when, after looking at my website, Paul had chosen more than forty shots he wanted to use!

I burned the shots to a disk so that he could have time to narrow down his choices.

My office has a waiting room, and that room is my "public gallery." As he was leaving, I pointed to a landscape shot I'd taken near Cape Town and said that, while I thought it was good, Galen Rowell probably would have done it better. Paul turned to one of the portraits and said, "That might be true, but no one in Nashville could have taken that shot." ("Eyes of Shiva" pictured on page 27).

I believed Paul meant what he said, but I had little idea what he'd seen in the shot that had prompted him to say it.

***

A relatively short time later, I had the opportunity to meet with the owner of one of the galleries in downtown Nashville. Since I had never done this before, I went there with my laptop, and as a means of looking at my work, we viewed my website (www.bobshermanphotography.com). She was most generous with her time, and she threw me my next curve ball. She told me that I had such a vast wealth of material and subject matter that, while she would certainly be interested in a show of my work, she was not at all certain what would be the best content or even context for that show.

"I thought my job was to take the shots, and your job was to do the selection," I said. She told me that, in my case, she wanted me to come back when I knew what kind of show I wanted to have.

Paul's response, as well as the gallery owner's, forced me to begin to question why I take photographs. They forced me to try to understand why I had so much difficulty in perceiving myself as a photographic artist. I needed to understand what exactly I was trying to communicate in my photography. Until that moment, I had never realized that my quest as a photographer and my quest as a therapist are the same endeavor. For now I will characterize that quest as the pursuit—for myself, my psychotherapy clients, and the viewers of my images—of a realization of who we really are and what is really important. I also believe that a direct experience of connection with that reality is possible.

***

The picture of the hands on page 10 is titled "Youthful Senectitude." I took it in Band-I-Amir, Afghanistan, in August 1975. Band-I-Amir is located in the Hindu Kush Mountains in central Afghanistan. It is about seventy-five kilometers from Bamyan. Bamyan was once the site of massive Buddhas carved into a mountain. The Taliban blew them up. I was most fortunate to have been able to visit these two places in 1974 and again in 1975. In those days, getting to these places required young bodies. The only ways to get there were by truck or van. These vehicles traveled on "roads" that were closer to lunar landscapes than to any intentional path of travel. By the time I'd arrived in Bamyan, my internal organs felt rearranged, and spare vertebrae would have been quite useful. I was able to climb to the top of the Buddhas and stand on their heads. I have no idea how anyone could consider the world a better place after these incredible carvings were destroyed.

I believe that there are six lakes in this area. Despite the desert-like setting, the lakes were wonderfully clean and amazingly cold. Each lake was a different shade of blue or green that didn't look real.

Band-I-Amir had no hotels. A strip of shack-like buildings offered a place where you could get a straw cot to sleep on. The only hot water available was from a tank that was heated by a cooking fire on the other side of the wall. In 1974 and 1975, Band-I-Amir was one of my favorite places in the world.

Regarding the photo that I took there, I like to ask people how old they think the person attached to the hands is. Most people will guess somewhere between sixty and seventy-five, but the girl these hands belong to is nine years old. That's why my name for that shot is "Youthful Senectitude." Senectitude means old age, or the final stage of life. I had met this girl walking with her brother, her mother, and one other woman. I took this shot as well as one of her brother's bare feet. I assure you that his feet are just as "old" as her hands. Her hands quite accurately reflect the realities of their existence. Light years cannot measure the distance between her life expectations and those of many American children, who believe that the minimum daily requirement of life starts with the latest iPhone.

The image "Glorious" on the preceding page is one of the lakes of Band-I-Amir and the surrounding countryside. Hotel Row was located just below the mountain on the top right in the photo. I

GLORIOUS - BAND-E-AMIR, AFGHANISTAN, 8/75

took the following shots of the horsemen on the flat ground between the mountains. I also took the photo of the young girl's hands here. The landscape is stark and unencumbered. While there, I could walk by myself in any direction and never have even a fleeting thought of danger. I don't have the ability to articulate what it's like to walk there at night. The lack of lights allows one to see forever into the sky. The first time I was there, I didn't know any Farsi, but that wasn't ever a problem. I quickly came to realize that if I showed an Afghan respect, he returned at least an equal amount with ease. And incidentally, it is never appropriate to call an Afghan an Afghani. The word *Afghani* is used to refer to their currency. They never refer to themselves as Afghanis.

One day in Bamyan, I noticed a nomad tribe heading towards the outskirts of town. The following morning, I walked in the same direction hoping to find them. As I entered their camp, three men called to me in Farsi and told me to go away. Initially, I ignored them. They picked up rocks. I then turned to them and greeted them in Farsi. Prior to this event I had lived in Iran for eleven months, and during that time I was able to learn enough Farsi to have at least rudimentary conversations. The Farsi in Afghanistan is purer and more ancient than the Iranian Farsi. Tehran is a far more modern city than anything in Afghanistan, so it has many more Western aspects and articles in its culture. Whenever there isn't a word in Farsi, the Iranians substitute the French word. But the two versions are close enough, so I could communicate. The guys motioned as if they were going to throw rocks at me again, so I spoke the ritual greeting common there. That greeting begins simply with, "Hello. How are you?" One can also include other phrases that don't translate well, for example, *I sacrifice myself for you*, or, *Your feet on my eyes*. The men dropped the rocks and decided to take me on a tour of their camp. They gave me *carte blanche* to take any photos I wanted. Near the end of my visit, I was talking with eight men about life. One of them asked me where my camera had been made?

How in the world do I explain where Japan is?

I took a stick and sketched a map of Afghanistan on the ground. I then drew all the countries to the East until I got to Japan. The one question that stumped me was, "How much did the camera cost?" How could I possibly tell this man that the "toy" around my neck cost more then he might have in five years? I punted on the question by merely saying, "a lot," and we all laughed. The photo on page 22 was taken in the nomad camp.

The two photographs after the nomad camp, "Buzkazee" and "Three Horsemen," are of Afghanistan's national game. In *Buzkazee* "the ball" is a dead goat. If you look carefully at the rider on the right in the front of the pack, you will see the goat lying transverse across the horse. The idea of the game is to grab the goat and take it to your goal. The locals told me that when the game is played in earnest, the only way to really see it is on horseback, and the game can sometimes last for days. I took these shots while standing in the middle of the playing field.

Just as I had with the picture of the girl on the carousel, I took these images using the technique called panning. That's why the background in the group shot is so blurry. The blur is also why, even though there are only two riders in the second photo, I named it, "Three Horsemen."

NOMAD CAMP - BAMIYAN, AFGHANISTAN, 8/75

THREE HORSEMEN - BAND-E-AMIR, AFGHANISTAN, 8/75

BUZKAZEE - BAND-E-AMIR, AFGHANISTAN, 8/75

I named the photograph that Paul had pointed to in my waiting room, "Eyes of Shiva" (page 27), and it is one of my favorite images. I took it in Rishikesh, India, in February 2003. The eyes of Indian people fascinate me. Indian eyes often appear as deep pools. Parents frequently apply charcoal to children's eyes to ward off the "evil eye." This gives them stark beauty. This boy stares at us through his penetrating brown eyes from a deep well of innocence. He has no difficulty in staring, or being stared at. He has no fear or concern about what you might see or judge as you look as deeply into his being as he looks into yours. The three stripes on his forehead indicate that he is a follower of Shiva and symbolize that he had gone through a prayer ceremony that morning.

A common misconception about Hindus is that they believe in thousands of Gods. This is actually not true. A fundamental precept of Hinduism is that only one God, Brahman, exists. However, Hinduism breaks down God into different attributes. A separate God symbolizes each attribute. The first division of God is into three parts: Brahma, Vishnu, and Shiva. Brahma symbolizes God as the creator. Vishnu symbolizes God as the preserver of the universe. Shiva is the destroyer, the agent of change, and as such, at the end of each great cycle, he destroys the universe in order that it may begin anew.

Starting with the next chapter, I will attempt to outline some of the significant components that led me to take those pictures in Afghanistan at age twenty-nine. I'm interested in describing who I thought I was, how I conceptualized my life, and how much shame influenced that conception. Throughout my life, I have had moments in which I was astounded by how out of touch I had been with things that were either staring me in the face or punching me in the stomach—or lower. For example, at age twenty-nine, I had no conscious idea that I had experienced any form of sexual abuse or that I was capable of using a camera to produce an image that was more than just a snapshot.

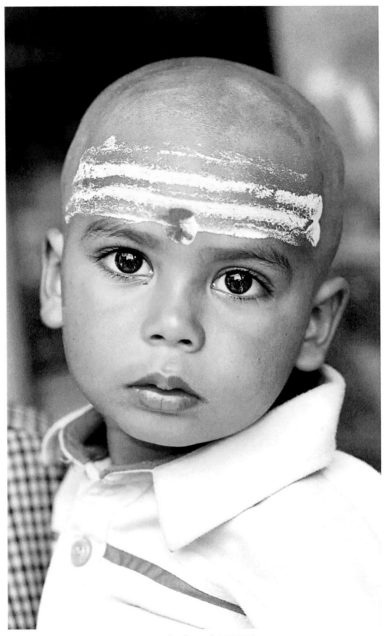

EYES OF SHIVA
RISHIKESH, INDIA, 2/03

CHAPTER THREE
Bobby

I was born on August 2, 1946, in Astoria, Queens in New York City. We lived on the third floor of an apartment building. My father was a tool and die maker. I don't know whether my mother was working outside our home at that time. I had one older brother, Ritchie. (There really isn't a "t" in his name; it's just how I've spelled it all my life.) He was six years older than me, and when I grew older, I often told people that my brother was an only child. I intentionally said it to get a laugh. I was not implying that he was narcissistic, because he was not. Underneath the joke was the reality that each of us was in it alone for much of our lives.

Our age difference was part of the reason that as kids we didn't really share much with each other. We often got into heated arguments. These arguments escalated until I was in my thirties, when our relationship took a wonderful turn for the better.

We never had any type of physical confrontation when we were kids. What we did have was a competitiveness that played itself out in golf and bowling when I was between the ages of fourteen and twenty-two. I started playing golf before Ritchie, but he eventually became a much better golfer than me. Bowling was another story. We had some wonderful matches. Most of the time it took at least a six hundred series to win. I'm fascinated that, as a teenager, I never thought of myself as a great bowler. The matches between Ritchie and me took place in a bubble, and neither one of us thought much about telling others about them. My parents never saw us bowl. My only desire was to beat my brother.

We had no way of knowing back then that we were so competitive with each other because we were desperate to earn our father's love. In reality, he was incapable of giving it to either of us.

My earliest memory is of standing in my crib and being unable to breathe. Later in life, I learned that I'd had the croup. Since I'd been born in the Middle Ages, doctors still made house calls. Dr. Shapiro gave me something to make me vomit—probably Ipecac. Once that happened, I could breathe again. I believe that my croup was gone by the time I was four.

Dr. Shapiro, was a cigarette smoking man of few words. He also treated my mother for her diabetes. When I was a little older, I learned that he wanted to prescribe something for Mom to relieve some of her anxiety. When she asked if he had something "natural," his response was, "Do you know where I can find a Valium tree?"

As a young child, I don't ever remember my father playing with me. My father and brother had a train set, but I was never allowed to play with it, because I was too young. When we moved from the apartment in Astoria that I'd lived in from birth to age five, I was just about old enough to play with it, but our new apartment didn't have room for the two sheets of plywood that my father used to nail down the tracks, so the train set disappeared from my life.

Two other memories from my childhood stick out. One happened when I was three or four. My brother and I were home alone—just imagine leaving a three year old and a nine year old home alone now—and we got in to an argument. I don't remember what it was about. What I do remember was that I had reached my limit, and I decided that I was "outta here." I packed a small gym bag with socks and very little else. I ran down the stairs and made a left turn to go to the corner. Once I reached the corner, a whole other reality came crashing down on me. I didn't have permission to cross the street. I stood there for quite a while and then trudged back home. I knew then that I was a loser.

The other vivid memory is of, again, being about four and walking down Crescent Street, feeling totally alone. I don't remember having any friends when we lived in Astoria. This deeply felt sense of loneliness became a central theme in my life and reinforced my perspective that I was a loser and perhaps there was something wrong with me.

***

As an adult I have come to cherish periods of solitude. For example, I like to travel and take pictures. I have made many trips to India. The first two were with my first wife. I took the next four trips alone. During those four, although I enjoyed the solitude, I often wished that I could share my experience with someone else. In 1999, I had the chance to share India with my then girlfriend and wife-to-be. What became clear was that, while I loved the time we spent together, the photographer in me would rather have been there alone.

Even though India is my favorite place to shoot, I have made several trips there without a camera. When I'm someplace with a camera, I find myself always looking for a shot. When I'm there without one, I am, to some extent, having a different experience. This may also be related to why I am not a good videographer. When I have a video camera in my hands, I'm still looking for "a moment," and I don't have a feel for capturing the flow. Alas, when I'm in a new environment without a camera, I'm still aware of the shots I would have taken.

Another enjoyable aspect of being in the world alone is finding myself viewing a gorgeous scene when no one else is around. I took the two landscape shots at the end of this chapter when I was completely alone. Frequently, landscape photographers will include someone in the shot for perspective. I believe that the inclusion of anyone in either of these would detract from the images.

Even in India, a country with 1.25 billion people, I have been alone on numerous occasions. But my predominant experience of being in India is to have too many people asking me too many questions. This can also work to my advantage, however. I have been to Varanasi at least nine times. When I was there in 1999 with my girlfriend, there were times when we became separated for some reason. All I had to do was stop what I was doing and turn to the nearest guy and ask, "Where is she?" and he would immediately know whom I was talking about and where she was.

***

Just before my sixth birthday, we moved to Clearview Gardens, a massive apartment complex in Whitestone, Queens. Garden apartments are two-story buildings—somewhat like town houses—that stretch in very long rows. All the apartments are attached to each other except for an occasional driveway to the parking lots behind the buildings. Each floor is a separate apartment that has either one or two bedrooms. We lived on the first floor in a two-bedroom apartment that had a living room, kitchen, and bathroom.

I lived here from the age of five to twenty. This was a new community, so the schools were not yet completed. By seventh grade, I had already attended six schools.

Clearview was an okay place to grow up; it was safe, and I had a few friends.

I had a tremendous amount of freedom and a frightening lack of supervision. As a child, I never thought about this. Whatever we grow up with becomes our normal. I have been working since I was eleven years old. I began earning money by washing cars, mowing lawns and babysitting. The money was mine to spend as I pleased.

At age twelve, one of my neighbors offered to teach me how to play golf. I asked my father if it was okay. After he said yes, it never occurred to me to ask him for the $75 I would need for clubs. I just went out and earned it. When I needed some gear, I would take a forty-five-minute bus ride to Flushing and then take a thirty-minute train ride to Manhattan to get whatever I needed. No one asked me where I had been or what I had been doing. My job was to have my rear end in my chair at six for dinner. As long as I did that, I could do whatever I wanted.

Most of the time, I went to play golf by myself. Occasionally, I would play with my neighbor, and when I was about sixteen, my brother and I would play, but these were the exceptions. I would practice by myself on a small patch of grass in the parking lot behind our apartment, and I would go to a nearby public course to play. Golf is usually played in foursomes, so the person in charge at the first tee would put me in with three strangers. I enjoyed being able to hit the ball farther than most of the people who played with me. My best round occurred when I was sixteen and a senior in high school. I was playing in a foursome with Eddie, the number one guy on our high school team. The golf gods were with me that day, and I shot a seventy-six. Eddie shot a seventy-five, and it was the most fun I've ever had playing golf. Playing with Eddie prompted me to concentrate in a very different way. Sadly, my game deteriorated over time, and my level of frustration increased to the point where I gave up the game at twenty-two. Before giving it up, I took some lessons, but, unfortunately, the "pros" who were my teachers didn't know what they were doing. The escalating arguments with my brother on the course also helped me to make the decision to retire from golf.

***

On my twelfth birthday, I experienced what was perhaps the best "gotcha" moment with my father. For many months I had been annoying him by repeatedly saying, "I want to drive." Finally, he took me in his 1954 stick shift Ford to a street in College Point, Queens. As we drove there, he let me know that he was going to give me an opportunity to realize my foolishness so that I would stop bothering him. He pulled the car over to the side of the road, and, with some fanfare, got out and told me to get behind the wheel and drive. He was quite pleased with the certitude of my failure. I got behind the wheel and looked at him one last time to make sure that this was not a joke. When he again said, "Okay, wise guy, drive!" I put the car in first gear and drove away. I can still hear him screaming, "Stop the car!" I had shifted into third gear and was approaching forty miles per hour at that point. I pulled over to the side of the road and got back into the passenger seat. We did not have a discussion about how amazing it was that I could drive without any lessons, and my father did not apologize for underestimating my abilities. In fact, we didn't have a discussion at all. I must admit that I really didn't feel the need for a discussion. I remember that moment as one of the only times my father didn't immediately vaporize my success.

***

My parents were both first generation American Jews. Their parents were fairly religious, but neither of my parents went to Synagogue nor did they practice their faith. I suspect that my mother didn't practice only because she didn't know how to stand up to my father's negative attitudes about religion. My father would frequently say that, "God is where you find Him, so I don't have to go to *shul* (synagogue)." Many of my neighbors were Jewish. The Jewish High Holy days consist of two holidays: Rosh Hashanah and Yom Kippur. On those days, many of my neighbors would go to the Clearview Jewish Center, but my parents never did. When I was eight years old, I started going to Temple on my own, but I didn't fully understand what was happening. I would mouth some of the words and sing the songs. My parents never asked me why I went, and fortunately they also didn't stop me. At that age, I would not have been able to articulate a reason.

As a young adult, I started to become aware of a dull ache in my abdomen. For a long time I interpreted that ache as somehow related to my fucked up childhood. I was wrong about that one. I now believe that that ache was my soul's desire to be re-united with God. That ache was my visceral reaction to lacking a directly felt sense of connection with the divine.

Judaism has never fed me spiritually. As that child, I did not feel close to God during services. Most of the time, it seemed to me that the Rabbis were trying to see how fast they could get through the service. People were always talking in the back of the room, too, and I could never figure out why they were there. As I grew older, I couldn't understand starting a prayer by saying, "I thank God that I wasn't born a woman." I realize that there is much more to Judaism than this. I'm also fairly certain that if I had been exposed to the more mystical components of Kabbalah I would have much that resonated within me. So I am not knocking or criticizing those who Judaism does feed. I may have just not gone to the right Jewish restaurants.

I don't really practice any religion. As my perceptions of guilt, shame, and self worth have transformed over the years, my spirituality has become a directly felt connection with something greater than myself. I have felt this connection in many different environments and with many different religious traditions—and sometimes with actions or experiences that have nothing to do with any religion at all. In a way, my credo might sound like an echo of my father's: *God is where you find Him.* The difference is that my father acted as if he thought he was God, and he didn't go looking. I pray that I don't act like I think I'm God, and I'm always looking.

I have come to refer to myself as a "Hinjew." I first heard this term from a man named Ram Dass, born Richard Alpert. Richard was also a psychologist, who did a lot of LSD trips with Timothy Leary in the 1960s while he was at Harvard. Richard Alpert became Ram Dass after his guru in India gave him that name. Ram Dass means servant of God.

Judaism has certainly been a valued aspect of the culture in which I was raised. Family, education, civil rights, and a liberal orientation are very much a part of who I am.

While I am not a practicing Hindu, India has certainly been the most influential environment for my spiritual growth. Varanasi is the holiest city in India, and it is the place where I feel closest to God. The philosophical underpinnings of Hinduism and Yoga have become the cinderblocks of my spiritual foundation, and they have allowed me to make sense out of existence. They also form the unspoken basis regarding my perception of who and what I'm relating to in my clients.

When I was thirteen, I went to a fundraiser that had a "Wheel of Chance." I put $1 down and I prayed. I don't remember ever having prayed before, and I gave it everything my thirteen-year-old heart and soul had. I won and left there with a brand new basketball. My sixty-five-year-old connection with God does not include the ability to control the outcome of Titans games, so don't call me. However, as a thirteen year old, I was impressed with my small miracle.

***

Every so often, my father would give me a spanking. These spankings had an order to them, and I knew it well. If my father wasn't home, my mother would write out a citation about what I had done. Then she'd say, "Wait until your father gets home."

When he arrived home, he'd ask, "Do you know what you did wrong?" Once I'd given the appropriate answer, he would tell me to remove my pants, and he would use his right hand to make a considerable impression on my rear end.

Once when I was seven and he was putting me over his knees, I said to myself, *not this time*. Despite my father's best efforts, I did not cry. That was the last time he ever spanked me.

I did not cry again until I was twenty-three, when I had what was to be the first of four knee surgeries. This was 1969 and before the advent of arthroscopic techniques. I am pretty sure my surgeon used a chainsaw for the procedure.

After the surgery, he came into my room.

"Raise your leg," he said.

I gave it everything I had, but the pain and muscle weakness prevented me from getting my leg off of the bed. My surgeon was undeterred. He lifted my leg and held it in the air.

"I am going to let go of your leg," he said, "and I want you to stop it from hitting the bed."

My knee felt like someone had turned it into a shish kabob using a dull spear. My surgeon just nodded.

"Raise your leg ten times every hour," he said, and left me there writhing in the gift of my pain.

He put me on some morphine shots for my pain. The nurses told me that I could have a shot every six hours. At exactly six hours, I would ring and ask if I could "please have a shot." Anywhere from thirty to seventy minutes later, a nurse would come in and let me know that I was turning myself into an addict by asking for shots so often and that I was being a wimp. The second day I was there just happened to be Christmas Eve. That evening some nurse made an announcement that we all shouldn't bother to ring for anything, because "no one was coming." I wish it had been a joke. I listened to a man on a gurney in the hallway in agony all night.

The following morning, I phoned my doctor's office and had him paged. I felt guilty about paging him on Christmas. About an hour later, my phone rang, and it was my surgeon. As I started to tell him that I hadn't had a shot all night, I found myself unable to talk because I was sobbing. I was shocked and unprepared for my tears. It took a while for me to be able to speak, and fortunately my surgeon waited. When I told him that I had never asked for a shot in less than six hours, he was aghast. He told me that I should have been getting shots every four hours. He immediately took me off the morphine injections and put me on a synthetic opiate pill (Percocet) for my pain, and Valium for my extreme muscle tension from my physical and emotional pain. He also told me that there was no way that I was becoming an addict. Within twenty-four hours, I was able to walk the hallways of the hospital.

Unfortunately, this incident did not permanently break the dike holding back my tears. That would have to wait until my forties when I bought a few therapists new cars after many sessions of not only relearning how to cry but also relearning who I was. Just as unfortunate is the fact that I would have to go through a few more prolonged experiences of pain in order to get to the point of cracking in other areas of my life. I now realize that my pain tolerance served me exceedingly well when I was a powerless child with no option of leaving. That same tolerance for pain did not serve me so well when I became an adult and had choices but continued to let myself feel powerless and trapped. However, I also fully realize that the pain in my adulthood was the only way I could get to the point of cracking, and that point was a most glorious opportunity for growth into a more compassionate perspective of myself and of the world.

***

My perspective as a child was that I had an internal sense of being different. Prior to third grade, I don't remember having any friends. I knew something was either wrong or unlikeable about me.

I knew I was smart, because I got good grades. I knew I could talk unusually well for a person my age.

***

Say Yes To Life.
Say Yes To Love.
Say Yes To Fun.
Say Yes To God.

Say Yes When I Ask You
If You Have
Cindy Crawford's Phone Number

(My holiday card 1995)

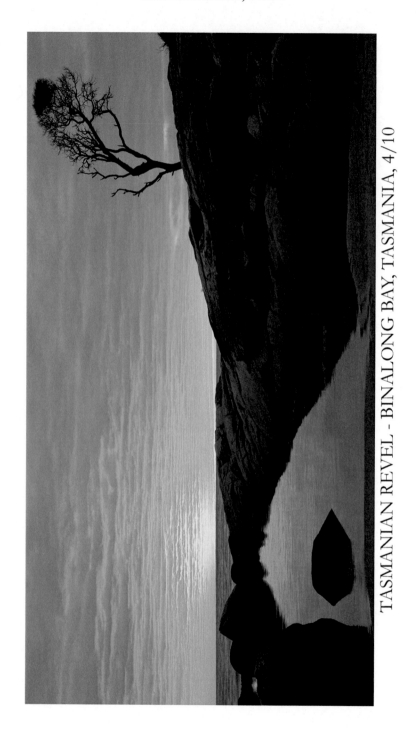

TASMANIAN REVEL - BINALONG BAY, TASMANIA, 4/10

BEGINNING - PRICETOWN, AUSTRALIA, 4/10

I took the image on page 42, "Tasmanian Revel," in Binalong Bay. Tasmania is an Australian island 240 kilometers south of the mainland. The name Tasmania may sound alien and exotic, but it's not a third-world country by any means. I got around in a rented Honda rather than a yak with a cart.

The weather haunted me all through my travels in Australia. I'd drive and or hike a long distance only to have the clouds come in and ruin my shot.

That was almost the case on the morning I took this picture, but that day my perseverance paid off. I arrived at Binalong Bay about an hour before sunrise. For me, and for many other photographers, the time for landscape photography is from about thirty minutes before sunrise to about thirty minutes after it, and from about one hour before sunset to about forty-five minutes after. These are the times when the light is most conducive to great images. The color of natural light changes throughout the day. Daylight is only really "white" when the sun is overhead. White light is rarely conducive to great images. In order to get a three-dimensional aspect to a landscape shot, a photographer needs to have shadows. There are no shadows on the landscape when the sun is overhead. As the sun gets closer to the horizon, the color of the light changes. It tends to be somewhat purple before sunrise and then turns yellow-orange. In the afternoon, the light grows progressively more yellow, then orange, and then red. The degree of these color shifts is a function of latitude, water vapor, and pollution or dust in the air.

So there I was at Binalong Bay, and the sky was the same murky grey that had haunted me for days. The weird tree had fascinated me when I'd first seen it. As I was getting ready to leave, the clouds parted just seconds before sunrise, revealing this gorgeous moment in the sky that was mirrored in the pond in the foreground. I was the sole person there. I did not enhance the colors in the image; this is how it really looked. But such moments are often fleeting. Thirty seconds after I took this shot, the sun rose into the clouds, and the magic was gone.

I also took "Beginning," shown on page 43, just before sunrise. The 12 Apostles is a major tourist attraction on the southern coast of Australia near Melbourne. I arrived there about an hour before sunrise and was alone under a gorgeous, star-filled sky.

I was so hopeful about the lighting director's choice for that morning until the clouds started rolling in on cue. But, again, I got very lucky. Before the clouds ruined the moment, I was able to take this shot. The dark blue and purple shades in the water are as true in the photograph as they were in nature.

As I've previously written, human vision is not an objective process. Very often we don't see things as they are. Instead we see things as we know them to be. The "silky" aspect to the water is a result of a time exposure. If the exposure is long enough, the movement of the water combines with the extended exposure to create this softened texture.

Both of these images portray an aspect of unadorned nature absent of any toxic waste. No power lines or any other signs of a human footprint altered the scene. I feel a sense of awe and gratitude in these places.

CHAPTER FOUR
My Mother

My mother was born around 1914, and she was the second youngest of four children. She had two brothers and a sister. I don't know how far she got in school or if she had a middle name. I do know that family was very important to her and that she loved my brother and me with all that she had.

I believe that one of my mother's passions as a child was dancing and that a knee injury prevented her from pursuing it further. I don't remember ever meeting my maternal grandfather, and I have no idea what he did for a living. I'm pretty sure that he abused alcohol. I did meet my maternal grandmother, but that's about all I remember of her. I'm astounded at how little I actually know about my mother, but my ignorance was no accident.

The Mary Sherman whom I knew when I was a child was someone to be tolerated. Her *job* was to cook, clean up the house, and keep quiet. These rules were never overtly stated. However my father's attitudes, feelings and behaviors were so pervasive that my brother and I couldn't help but be swept

away by his tide of righteousness and superiority.
Sadly, we adopted the same stance towards her. I
was in my twenties when a change in my perspective
allowed me to develop a more compassionate and
appropriate relationship with my mother. I was
starting to think somewhat independently from my
father's indoctrination. As a result, I was able to
recognize some of my father's inappropriate
behavior, and this allowed me to perceive my
mother differently.

***

When I was a child, Ritchie used to taunt me
with, "You should have been a girl." This was not
his way of suggesting that I was gay; it was his way
of reacting to knowing that before I was born, my
mother had given birth to a baby girl who had died
shortly after birth. My mother also gave birth to one
stillborn baby and had some miscarriages. I have no
idea how many. I cannot imagine her pain and
sorrow. I also cannot imagine my father being
present for her as a source of comfort. I am certain
that he buried the pain and sorrow of these tragic
losses so deeply within himself that he had no
comfort to offer.

My mother was also pregnant before she and my
father got married. In order for my father to gain
approval from his own parents to marry my mother,
he had to convince her to get an abortion. I shudder
at the image of my perhaps nineteen-year-old
mother in the 1930s getting an abortion. I also

speculate that my mother was sexually abused as a child. I base my speculation only upon a few educated guesses. My mother must have had her own shame issues. What else would have prompted her to tolerate my father's abuse? Often sexual abuse survivors marry other survivors or individuals who themselves grew up in environments where boundary violations were the norm. I have no idea how my mother was able to function as well as she did with all the devastation that she carried within herself. Despite her losses, she was able to raise her children, keep her home spotless, maintain a job, and not let anxiety or depression consume her.

At the time she became pregnant with me, my mother was on a medication named DES because of complications after her previous delivery and multiple miscarriages. The DES was supposed to make her infertile. I am the accident that indicates she wasn't as infertile as her doctor had thought. I know that my mother was overjoyed that I came into her life. She was very quick to tell me this whenever she would overhear my brother taunting me. My father's reaction to my conception, however, must have been quite different. He viewed me as yet another cross to bear in his existence.

***

My father made it very clear to the universe that he viewed my mother as the key obstacle to him reaching his full potential. Sometime before Ritchie was born, my father separated from my mother and moved out to the West Coast. My father told me that he came back to her because of his profound sense of responsibility. However, as the years went by, he let anyone who would listen know that the only reason he stayed with her was because of this immense sense of responsibility. He'd stayed just because he was that great of a guy.

Sadly, his saintliness did not prevent him from inundating us with his anger that let us know that the three of us were his collective albatross. My mother died in 1981. As soon as my father got back to their apartment after her death, he couldn't wait to throw out anything and everything that was hers. Ritchie and I had to stop him from doing this. My father celebrated finally "getting out of jail." He started to travel, and he made his relationships with other women public. His freedom was short-lived, however. Nine months later, he was dead. It seems the guy just didn't know how to live without his ball and chain.

***

My mother's domain was our apartment. She tried to run a tight ship in terms of everything being tidy and clean. Up until the day I moved out at age twenty, I could regularly hear my mother screaming, "Bobby pick up your clothes!" I never picked them up. I'm sure I was just behaving passive aggressively. I knew she couldn't tolerate the sight of whatever clothing I had dropped. She just had to pick it up, put it in the hamper, wash it, fold it, and put it in my dresser. So I knew that whatever it was, it would be there when I needed it. If she had only let it lay there, I would have eventually needed it. I'm sure that if she had ever done that, my initial response would have been to get angry with her for not "doing her job." But if she had just said nothing I would have learnt my lesson.

If somewhere in the universe she is listening, I'd love for her to get a laugh at how I finally did learn my lesson. I moved out at the age of twenty to move in with my girlfriend. On Friday nights I would lie around on our pullout sofa bed in the "living room." Since this was a studio apartment, I'm using the term living room quite loosely. Friday nights were for lying in bed and watching *Star Trek* while eating cheese danishes. (One of the major themes of my existence has been the pursuit of the ultimate cheese danish.) So there I was, engrossed in my sugar Trekkie wonderland, and the next thing I knew, my girlfriend was standing in front of me blocking my view of the TV. As I began to articulate my righteous indignation, she picked up the undershorts that were lying on the floor in front of the bed.

"If you want anymore of this," she said while grabbing one of her gorgeous breasts, "there will be no more of that." She dropped the offending item back on the floor.

There is a concept in the behavioral sciences termed "one trial learning." This should be the example used in the texts. The sixteen or so years of my mother's screaming did not accomplish what that one gesture did. Since that moment, I have never left anything lying around—even in the absence of those breasts.

***

I know very little about my mother's relationships with her siblings. I believe that their birth order was her older brother, Maxie; her sister, Ann; my mother; and her younger brother, Kelly. Maxie and Kelly were both New York City Firemen, and I believe that they were also both in the Navy during World War II. As a child, I'd had very little contact with Maxie or Kelly and their respective families. Despite this, I do have very fond memories of Kelly. We used to call him Uncle Mushy, and I have no idea why. But in another one of these latent synapses-firing moments, I have a clear memory of being perhaps three or four and Uncle Mushy letting me "drive" his car by putting me on his lap and letting me steer. Kelly and Ann both died before my mother passed away. I have no idea about Maxie and his family. Ann's death was very difficult for my mother.

Ann was married to Simon, who had come from Austria and still had a thick accent. He worked as a frisket cutter, a guy who carves letters for signs. I imagine that computer-driven robots do that now. Ann and Simon were the only members of my mother's family that I had any contact with after we'd moved to Clearview. Ann was the first person to take me to a Broadway show. Simon introduced me to art and painting. Simon tended to be angry

about life. In his later years he told me about people
and "their religion." "They wear a cross around their
necks but don't cover their mouths when they
sneeze. What kind of religion is that?" he said. Ann
was always prim and proper and spoke a form of
"refined" English.

My father did a great job of isolating us from
much of our extended family. Yet he "allowed" my
mother the most contact with Ann. Ann and Simon
lived on the Grand Concourse in the Bronx. One
Thanksgiving my father and I went to the Bronx to
pick them up to bring them to our apartment for our
Thanksgiving celebration. I was probably thirteen or
fourteen at the time. Ann answered the door wearing
only a skirt and a bra. As a thirteen-year-old, I was
quite surprised at her nonchalance. My father
seemed nonplussed, however. It is only now as I
reflect on this memory that I believe Ann and my
father might have had an affair.

***

My mother asked me a lot of questions. At times,
I felt like she was sucking the life out of me. As a
shrink, I now call it engulfment. I felt a pain in my
chest at these times and a strong desire to escape.
Her suffocation aroused anger within me. In the
Sherman family, it was permissible to get angry with
my mother. Getting angry with my father, however,
was quite another story. My mother also had no
concept of appropriate boundaries. As a teenager, I
never knew when she might walk into my bedroom

without knocking. That also added to my breathing difficulties.

I am grateful that as I grew older I was able to create a more compassionate and loving relationship with my mother. This shift in perspective was powerful enough to open the possibility for larger shifts to come. She passed away just as our relationship was getting much better. The sadness I feel for the time I wasted being angry with her serves as a perpetual catalyst for remembering to always look for ways to accept a more loving and compassionate worldview.

What did I know about my mother? Up until about the time I turned nineteen, I knew that my mother was a pain in my ass. I knew that she asked too many questions. I knew that she made sufficient quantities of food and two great cakes. I knew that she loved me. I also knew that she never told me that my father's behavior was inappropriate.

***

Have You Noticed That
Loving Often Feels As Good
Or Better Than Being Loved?

Who Are You Hurting By
Withholding Your Capacity
To Show That Love?

(My holiday card 2003)

CHAPTER FIVE
My Brother Ritchie

Richard Alan Sherman was born in Astoria, Queens in 1940. I have no idea what the environment was like into which Ritchie was born. No two children really have the same parents. First-born children usually have the full attention of their parents. Subsequent children have to share in the amount of attention they receive. Frequently the relationship of the parents changes over time. Quite possibly Ritchie greatly resented my intrusion into his world, given the scarcity of any positive attention from my father.

Sometime during his childhood, Ritchie suffered a collapsed lung that required surgery. Ritchie also suffered from asthma. He was six years older than me. This is a good example of how perception can shape every aspect of your universe, because it's clear that both Sherman offspring had a difficult time breathing and knew the terror of possible suffocation.

Ritchie and I didn't really do much with each other until I was about thirteen. That's when we started competing in sports, and we were never more competitive than when we played golf. Although some of our matches were wonderful, many of our golf outings were punctuated with intense arguments. Our last golf argument took place outside of his apartment. We were arguing over what had taken place on the course.

"I don't give a shit about what you think happened," Ritchie said. "I told you what happened, and you can either agree, or we have nothing more to talk about."

I put my clubs in my car and ended the conversation. This led to a fairly long period of cordiality between us at family functions but no real interaction.

This "divorce" was very difficult for my mother, and each of us received fairly frequent phone calls from her. "You need to call your brother," she'd say. Ironically, her death is what began the process of bringing us back together. I'm heartbroken that she never got to see how close we ultimately became.

During my childhood, I came to view myself as the favored child. It seemed to me (at that time) that I got far less grief from my father than Ritchie did. When I was forty-five, resurfacing memories in therapy sessions shattered those illusions. In those sessions, I began to cry when I remembered how my father had mistreated my brother. I was out of touch with the fringe benefits of my favored status.

For most of his life Ritchie struggled with his weight. He was never obese, but sadly he was not blessed with the same ridiculously active metabolism that I have. For Ritchie and me, food became love, comfort, and anesthesia. To this day, I still eat too much food. At sixteen, I was working as a clothing store salesman and stock boy, and I would head to a nearby Chinese restaurant, sometimes ordering and eating dinner for three.

Ritchie was far more active in high school than I was. He was a saxophone player in the school's hip quartet, The Commodore Cats. He also played basketball for his college team. I don't know why we never brought our competitiveness to the basketball court. It would have been fun. My guess is that I didn't realize how good a basketball player I was until my early twenties.

Originally Ritchie wanted to be an electrical engineer. He went to Brooklyn Polytechnic for a few years and then transferred to Queens College when he decided to become a math teacher. Ritchie was the kind of math teacher that you want your kids to have. He cared deeply about his students and gave far more than warranted by what he was paid. Ritchie's students learned about a lot more than math in his classes.

He got married, and he participated in raising two wonderful daughters. Though he and his wife divorced, they remarried a few years later. In my many years of practice, I have come to realize that it was not ironic that he seemed to replicate what our father had done. But I want to be clear that Ritchie was not at all like our father when it came to parenting or being a husband.

Ritchie never really seemed to embrace any spiritual path, so that is something that we had never really shared with each other. He was concerned with being a decent, loving, and giving human being. He had no desire to treat others as our father had. Ritchie made himself available to his students after school, and his garden was beautiful. He left the world he lived in a better place.

***

What perspectives did I have of my brother? As a child I knew that I had a brother who was a roommate who I would see at the dinner table. I knew that my father was disappointed with my brother. As a teenager I knew that I could compete with my brother as an equal in golf and bowling. In my twenties I perceived my brother as a schmuck, but by my mid-thirties, my experiences had expanded my perspective enough to realize that I had a brother who loved, respected, and in some ways looked up to me. I knew that we both were in the world trying to be the best that we could, and in many ways were living our lives in reaction to our parents. I loved my brother very much and I miss him a lot.

CHAPTER SIX
My Father

I think that Charles (Charlie) Bernard Sherman was born in 1915. His parents were immigrants from what was referred to in my family as Russia-Poland. He had an older brother named Joseph and two younger sisters. I know very little about my paternal grandfather, Louis. I remember him lying on a couch. I believe that he was very ill at that time, and he died shortly thereafter. I do have memories of my maternal grandmother, Rose. She and I had a relationship. I can remember playing a game of cards with her called *Pisha Pasha* (Yiddish for up and down). I can remember an incident when I was about eight, when I had called my mother crazy. Grandma immediately scolded me for "talking like that" to my mother. She suggested that I could instead say, "Mother, are you thinking correctly?" Somehow I don't think that my father had the same kind of relationship with his parents that I had with his mother.

Both of my parents grew up on the lower east side of Manhattan in the 1910s to the 1930s. That was where a lot of Jewish immigrants settled. To this day, remnants of that Jewish culture linger in the lower east side. Jonah Shimmel was the name of a bagel bakery there, and it became my nickname for my oldest son. His name is Jonas.

***

Charlie was a gymnast in high school. He had planned on getting a scholarship to college as a result of his skills. In either his junior or senior year, Charlie dislocated a shoulder, and that not only ended his gymnastics career, it also precluded him from going to college. I think that he wanted to become a lawyer. I also believe that he thought that his parents could have paid for his college and chose not to do so. He graduated with a trade school diploma instead, and he eventually became a tool and die maker.

Charlie's siblings were a most interesting mix. His older brother, Joey, became a truck driver. He was the street fighter in the family who often saved Charlie's butt. I'm fairly certain that Charlie's mouth often wrote checks that his fists could not cash. I'm also fairly certain that Charlie was not capable of showing Joey the appreciation that he deserved. I never heard my father say anything good about his brother. What I did hear were derogatory and sarcastic digs. My aunts informed me of Joey's pugilistic skills. All I really remember from my father was his disdain for his brother and that he flirted with Joey's wife.

Charlie's two sisters were Zeldy and Martha. Zeldy eventually married Leon, and, as a married couple, they were the only models I ever had of two people who loved and respected each other. Martha, the only remaining living member of that generation in my family, eventually became the first woman rehearsal pianist for the American Ballet Theatre. She had to be the rehearsal pianist because, even though she was a great pianist and a graduate of the Juilliard School of Music, at that time, women were not allowed in the pit (the orchestra that played the music for the performances).

Within the family, Martha had one other claim to fame. She married "Stretch." Stretch is the smartest person I've ever met. He was also a wonderful dancer; he danced with Lena Horn in the *Cotton Club*. He had a marvelous sense of humor. He was about six-feet-six-inches tall and he was black. This last, not-so-minor point did not go over so well with all of the family. Charlie's parents actually *sat shiva* for Martha after they disowned her. *Sitting shiva* is the ritual that Jews go through after someone dies. After that, the family was split, with her parents and Joey on one side and Zeldy and my father siding with Martha and Stretch.

During the 1930s, my father and Stretch were active in the trade labor movement. I believe that is where my father met Stretch. Charlie was quite good at sensitizing Ritchie and me to certain social issues; the plight of workers in America was one of them.

Sometime during the 1950s, Charlie went into management. He became a plant manager for some interesting factories. Detecto scales were great, I suppose; we were always weighed regularly. But Loft Candy was by far my favorite company that Charlie managed. Boxed candies of that ilk have a code built into them. The color and the swirl on top are no accidents. They are unique and are used to identify what is inside. So I never had that problem of biting into something, making a face, and then throwing it away; I knew exactly what my teeth were getting into. My father retired around 1980. He did not invite Ritchie or me to his retirement party. This saddened us but did not surprise us.

***

Much of what I have written about my father has been negative. I do want to note, however, that the lessons I learned from him weren't all bad. My father loved classical music, and because he was mechanically adept, he was able to build amplifiers (look up Heathkit), and he even designed our speakers. By the time I was eight, I could have passed any college level music appreciation course. I didn't know this until I had to take one as an undergraduate and never went to class. I just walked in and took the final. I also inherited my father's aptitude for mechanics. By the time I was eleven, I had already rebuilt the carburetor in our family car. I still enjoy fixing things. We did go on some family vacations, and that's how I was first introduced to travel. My father was also interested in photography and bought me my first camera.

My father was my idol until I was about fourteen. I looked like him. I talked like him. Many of my mannerisms were copies of his. However, once the shine started to fade, I quickly wanted to be nothing like him. Later in life, I had to learn that I could still like classical music and not be like him.

When I was twenty I became quite depressed. This prompted me to go into therapy for the first time. During this period of depression, I wrote some poetry. The following is a poem that I wrote about my father. It's interesting that all my other poems have titles, and this one does not. At the time that I wrote this poem, I consciously knew that the poem was about my father. Perhaps I was afraid of the consequences if he found out.

***

The climb of the vine
with insatiable hunger, unrest.
Always searching, ever lurching,
to make the final conquest.

It never asks, never takes.
Always the same slow steady crawl.
It never gives and only lives
on the goodness given by all.

And in the knowing where it is going
It never makes a mistake.
It encompasses all and there is its fall
for now it has only itself to partake.

CHAPTER SEVEN
Dinner

Much of our family drama played out during dinners. Since my mother was a typical 1950s housewife, dinner was ready when my father got home from work. That was usually at 6 p.m.

When I was between the ages of six and fifteen, if I wasn't "in trouble," I would eagerly await my father's arrival. I am aware now that my eagerness then was the equivalent of a cow fervently awaiting the arrival of a butcher. By the time I was six, I had honed my skills to the point where I could tell what kind of mood my father was in by the way he unlocked the door.

After he got home, my father would typically go into our kitchen and pour himself a shot of booze. My parents would engage in some small talk, and then my mother would call us to dinner. We had assigned seats. I sat to my father's left. My brother sat to his right, and my mother sat opposite my father with her back to the sink and stove.

My mother—*bless her heart*. A quick side note: The phrase "bless her heart" is very common in

Nashville. However, I have never heard it inside my head before—as I have just now—when thinking about her. *The natives may be getting to me.* Down here, people often follow the phrase *bless her heart* with a critical comment. Well, here goes, my mother—bless her heart—was not a very good cook. But she did know how to cook in sufficient quantities for the family. We always knew what was for dinner because she had a two-week rotating schedule.

After she served the food, my brother and I would unconsciously hold our breaths because, at that point, my father would ask one of us a question. The question could be about anything: school subjects, current events, politics or abstract concepts. He never asked both of us. He would ask the question and then turn to one of us for an answer. I never asked Ritchie about this moment for him, but I can assure you that when my brother was the one in my father's sights, I would breathe easy and prepare to watch the show. I also would inhale a ridiculously large amount of food as I watched from the safety of my position. One of the rules of this game was that you couldn't pass on answering the question. What didn't become clear to me until much later in life was that it really didn't matter what side of any issue we took; my father would always take the other side. If my father asked my brother the question, I spent the rest of dinner watching Pop demolish him. On other days, I was the one he badgered. But my father always inflicted one additional thing on my brother that he didn't on me. That was *the sigh*. He never gave me the sigh, and this was my proof that he favored me. Every so often, after hearing something either about Ritchie, or something Ritchie had just said, my father would let out this deep sigh as he shook his head from side to side. Just as the echo of the sigh faded he would then say, "When?" in a tone that clearly communicated a deep sense of frustration and disappointment. He didn't have to say the rest of the sentence, which was, *When are you going to stop being such a fuck up?* I really don't know why I never got a "when?" But I did get a few other things.

My father had one other rule in his dinner game. That rule was that my mother was never allowed to voice an opinion about the topic. Her job was to dish out the food and be quiet. If she ever made the mistake of offering an opinion, my dad would meet her with a glare.

My father did an excellent job of teaching us many different things, and, of course, fewer experiences shape a child's perspective more than the constant instruction of a dominant parent. Some of the lessons were clearly overt. Others were quite subtle but at least as powerful. One of the overt ones was to view my mother as something to be barely tolerated. As a child, I don't believe that I was ever consciously aware of how this perception of my mother affected me other than my almost constant experience of annoyance with her. When I started dating, I was neither disrespectful of my girlfriends nor did I treat them as second-class citizens. But I did treat them as beings whom I needed to take care of.

***

I did have some positive takeaways from my experiences at our family dinner table. My father's technique, as he often described it was to "give the other guy enough rope to let him hang himself." In order to do this, one has to be able to listen carefully and remember everything. These are pretty good talents for a therapist to have. Sadly, my father used his skills to demean and wield power over others. My father also modeled a fairly high level of sarcasm. Most New Yorkers have some sarcastic molecules floating around their blood stream, but Charlie was near the top of the food chain here. I must admit that I have an ambivalent relationship with my ability for sarcasm. As I've already stated, I'm still a work in progress. My perspective is forever shifting.

The skills that I learned at dinner came in most handy at the end of my schooling for my doctorate. The final test is called the "doctoral defense." The university appoints a committee of faculty members who evaluate the candidate's thesis. The committee then meets with the candidate, who defends his or her work, and other faculty who have helped with the dissertation. The doctoral defense either makes or breaks the student. At least that's the way it was when I was at NYU. The meeting lasts for about three hours, and then there is a vote. If the student passes, he or she becomes a doctor at that moment. If he or she fails, the student is out.

So with all of this in mind, I walked in to my defense. My chairman asked if anyone had anything to say. A youngish looking woman on my left immediately said, "Yes." She then added, "I am appalled that this committee ever allowed for this defense to take place today. It is apparent that whomever did the statistical analyses did not understand the underlying assumptions. I doubt very seriously that this meeting will have a successful conclusion."

I turned to her. "I was the one who did all of the statistical computations, and I will be more than happy to address all of your concerns." My veneer of confidence along with my debating skills served me exceedingly well during the next three hours. When the festivities had ended, the chair excused me from the room so that the vote could take place. So on April Fools Day 1974, I became Robert Sherman, Ph.D.

***

I'd like to share one more incident regarding my father because it is indicative of a pattern of events that led to me being profoundly out of touch with my wants and needs. When I was in sixth grade, I was rarely in my actual class, because I was a lieutenant on the safety patrol. I was in charge of all the audio-visual aids in the school. That meant that if a teacher wanted to show a film, I had to help. And when the secretaries went out to lunch, I answered the phones.

One day, one of the secretaries took me home for dinner as a way of thanking me. When she took me back home, she gave me a box of jellied candy. I can't tell you how much I loved getting that present. I even remember exactly what it looked like. I couldn't wait to get inside and show everyone my treasure. I got home as dinner was finishing, and my father immediately said, "Great, now we have dessert." Dread crept through me. I had never thought of a scene in which I would be watching my father and brother inhale my treasure. When I did not immediately and cheerfully hand over the candy, my father treated me to a long dissertation about what kind of selfish piece of crap I was. To this day, I often eat my food too quickly while slouching over my plate. And if I were to share what it's like for me to receive a gift, I'd have to write another book.

***

Every so often I would end our family dinners by angrily staring into my father's eyes. Then I would dramatically place my right elbow on the table with my hand in the air. This was the episodic challenge for arm wrestling. The room usually held a sense of levity at these moments, and I knew that in a matter of seconds my right hand would be lying face up on the wrong side of the success line. When I was fifteen, the unthinkable happened. The ritual started, but somehow my father's hand and arm ended up on the table with mine on top! My father never let me win, so I knew that I had indeed beaten him! I was in ecstasy until I looked at his face. He gave me an unmistakable glare that indicated I had done something very, very wrong. I quickly left the kitchen, and we never arm wrestled again.

***

Control is only an illusion
A shared moment is such a precious gift
The present needs to be fully savored
Because it is all we really have

Why is great cheese danish so hard to find?

(My holiday card for 2000)

CHAPTER EIGHT
School

Before college, school had always come easy to me. I was blessed with sufficient intellectual horsepower so that getting good grades wasn't too difficult, aside from my previously mentioned French escapades. The other major exception was that I cheated in seventh grade typing. I was in seventh grade in 1959. Back then, I could not see the relevance typing would have in my life, so I learned to type with two fingers fast enough to pass the course. As my two fingers do all the walking over my keyboard now, I think about how lovely it would be to type seventy words per minute without looking.

In 1959, the New York City school system instituted Special Progress classes. This meant that if your IQ was high enough you could skip eighth grade. I did, and that was a mistake. It isn't a good idea to be a sixteen-year-old senior in high school. I felt socially inept and too young for the really cool girls. That didn't stop me from becoming the president of my high school fraternity, however. It also didn't stop me from helping the school's number one thug pass eleventh grade math. That little feat made me untouchable to any and all undesirables; they knew that I was under "Denny's protection."

Eleventh year math was also significant in that I earned a ninety-seven percent as a final grade. I couldn't wait to get home and show my father. My father took one look at my report card and said, "What happened to the other three points?" Something snapped inside me at that moment, and I only earned a sixty-seven in geometry the following year. I did not let my grade slip with any conscious intent to "show" my father. I wasn't really aware of how devastated I felt about being three points short of acceptable. Still, that didn't stop me from graduating with a ninety-three percent average.

At the end of the eleventh grade, my father said to me, "There is no way that you're not going to college. And there's no way that I'm paying for it." There was never any further conversation about this. I do know that I was indeed looking forward to going away to school, but that option had just been removed. I never spoke to anyone else about this. My unconscious perspective was that it was my job to take care of whatever life presented me and whatever I wanted. Unfortunately, in my mind, asking for help was not an option. Since I wanted to go to college, I decided to go to Queens College of the City University. I knew that my grades were good enough, so I didn't apply to any other schools. It never dawned on me to go to my guidance counselor and find out about scholarships.

I was working at a clothing store all through high school, and that summer I started working as a waiter at a hotel in the Catskill Mountains. For those of you who might appreciate this, it was indeed a *schlock* house. Schlock house is a Yiddish term for a hotel in the Catskills that does not specialize in fine dining. Schlock houses are typically small. My hotel held about two hundred guests. Since food was included with the room cost, most of the guests felt compelled to make sure they got their money's worth at all meals. Just imagine a guest picking up the menu, looking at me, and only saying "yes."

There was just one minor speed bump in my plan. I was only seventeen, and a waiter needed to be eighteen to be employed at this hotel, so I borrowed a friend's driver's license, and for two years I was "Eddie Liebowitz." No one there ever knew my real name.

These hotels usually had three or four main dishes on the menu. The kitchen never made enough of any one of them to feed the entire dining room. The waiters were not allowed to eat the guest food. Instead, we ate in a special staff dining room. I'm not sure where that food came from. I am sure that it would not have won any awards. So I learned how to satiate myself with the forbidden guest food.

The last weekend of the season was Labor Day, and the last meal was Sunday lunch. Well this Sunday lunch did not go well, because *everybody* ordered the duck, and the kitchen ran out. A large number of irate guests gave the owners a hard time. When the last guest had finally left the dining room, the female owner, Sally, came over to my table to sit down and have a cigarette with me. (Just to show how times have changed, my birthday present from my parents for my fifteenth birthday was permission to smoke in the house.)

"Are you hungry," I asked.

She laughed and said, "yes."

"Well, what would you like to eat?"

In an exaggerated and frustrated tone she said, "Duck."

"Well, how many would you like?"

She gave me a look of total disbelief followed by another look that can only be translated as, *Are you fucking kidding me?*

I opened my serving table to reveal four main dishes of duck. All she could do was laugh. The two of us had a lovely meal. (This, indeed, was Charlie Sherman chutzpah at its finest). The next year, I returned as one of her favored waiters.

***

My first two years at Queens College were a waste of time. I rarely went to class, and I was somewhat depressed. I had no idea what I wanted to major in; these were the days before one went to college to major in sex and booze. I had a 1.75 average, and I should have been thrown out. I have no idea why I wasn't. In the second semester of my sophomore year, I took two courses that changed my life. One was experimental psychology, and the other was philosophy; both had excellent professors.

All of a sudden I found myself doing extra credit work for the psychology class. By the end of that semester, the professor asked me to be his research assistant, and my career in psychology began.

On the first day of the philosophy class, the professor walked in looking stoned. He looked like he was hallucinating. I don't know what was going on for him, but he turned me on to a wonderful world of ideas that enthralled me. I took every class that he taught.

My GPA went from a 1.75 in my first two years to a 3.75 in my last two years. By the time I had graduated, I knew that I wanted to get a Ph.D. and be licensed as a psychologist. I was lucky enough to get into NYU, and I graduated from there in 1974.

A few years later, I returned to NYU to take some additional classes. These classes were the subjects that I was truly interested in for my career. What a difference it was to be sitting in a class and not feel any pressure from the academic hierarchy. Whenever the professor chewed out another student, I could only laugh because I was finally done with that bullshit.

***

What did I know while in school? I knew life was going to present me with difficulties. It was my job to figure out what needed to be done and to just do it. It was my job to persevere no matter what it took. Despite the fact that I clearly had many competencies, my underlying perspective continued to convince me of my unworthiness. I never felt like the really cool women would be attracted to me. I knew that I felt lonely a lot. What I wasn't aware of was most of my wants, needs, and fears.

CHAPTER NINE
Sex: Part I

I can't think of any other aspect of my life than sex that has been such a profound source of both pain and pleasure. I also can't think of any other aspect of my life in which I have been more out of touch. I will do my best to share my experiences without revealing inappropriate information about my partners.

One of the positive aspects of the Charlie Sherman educational system was that, at a very early age, I was exposed to talking about things like compassion, sensitivity, values, and ethics. I remember being four and going to visit my father's parents in Coney Island. I spent some time playing with a girl in the apartment building who was the same age as me. All the adults were sitting outside on the sidewalk. When I came outside, my father asked me what I had been doing, and I told him that I had been playing with this girl. "She's very mature for her age," I said. I was shocked when everybody started laughing at me. I knew I was right. What I didn't know was that most four year olds don't talk about the maturity level of their peers.

Well, one of my father's most favored subjects in his curriculum for his sons was sex. All you need to know at this time is that the most powerful and frequent pronouncement from Daddy God was that, "Sexual intercourse is the ultimate expression of love between a man and a woman." I don't remember what about that I understood at four years old, but when I was about eight, I came to deeply believe it. I knew that whenever I was going to have intercourse, it would only happen if I knew that I was in love.

At twelve, I discovered sex with my right hand while watching bowling on TV; it came as a shock. A whole new reality opened up for me. I couldn't wait for a time when I could share the experience with a girl.

The Sherman school of communication techniques did not serve me well at the start of my dating career. I felt semi-paralyzed in regards to making the first move. I never knew the right thing to say. I didn't know how to turn down the tape in my head that constantly played the same message: *Why would she be interested in you?* So, Garry Hill, if you're still out there, I'm sorry that I never had the guts to ask you out. For the record, I still believe you would have said no.

Eventually, I did begin to date. If there is a category in the Guinness Book of World Records for saying no to intercourse for non-religious reasons, I'm sure that I'd get at least an honorable mention. I said no to all of my girlfriends because I knew that I didn't love them enough. My perspective was that if I had said yes, I would have been lying to them and taking advantage of them. Anything else was fine. This was back in the day before Howard Stern had invented anal intercourse, so I never even considered that as an option. This was also well before Bill Clinton had made it clear to the universe that oral sex wasn't sex. When I was in high school, we knew about oral sex, but unlike today, oral sex wasn't just a way of hooking up with someone who you just met at a party, so it was a relatively rare occurrence. However it did qualify on the "approved" list because it was not the "ultimate expression."

Around the age of seventeen, I started dating "Jane." Sadly, her previous boyfriend had recently raped her. This was the first relationship in which I was consciously aware of my desire to help a female overcome her self-perception of being damaged. I'm not sure I thought I was trying to "cure" her, but I was definitely there to provide a reality of safety and trust. Then one day she made it clear that my "treatment program" had been a success, and she'd like to have intercourse with me. True to my training, I thanked her but declined her most generous offer.

When I fell in love, I was nineteen. I worked as a waiter in a hotel in Pennsylvania. This one was not a schlock house, and it had a capacity for a large number of guests. A most gorgeous woman named Natasha worked at the front desk, and I initially thought she was out of my league. So I went out with a number of her friends and co-workers instead. By mid-summer, this woman had heard positive feedback about me. I believe that this allowed me to make my approach; we started talking and soon began dating. Natasha was not only gorgeous, she was also intelligent, a foreigner (Ukrainian Canadian), and had an abundance of experiences that were different from mine. She also had a wonderful voice.

I fell in love. I experienced her as a woman of depth, and she was clearly not just another girl. I wanted to spend as much time with her as I could. I wanted to know everything about her, and I wanted her to know me. We took a weekend off from work and went to a lake in New York. That night we were in our motel, and all systems were a go. At long last I had satisfied all the proper conditions. I was finally in love. Mere words cannot convey my devastation, inadequacy, confusion, and despair when I then learned the meaning of premature ejaculation. All I knew was that I had failed miserably and that I was most clearly defective. She was wonderfully kind and understanding, but that didn't take away the pain.

Despite this, we continued to date. When I went back to school in September, she stayed on to work because the hotel's season didn't end until October. In October, she moved to New York City, and we continued dating. Sadly, my premature ejaculation also continued.

One other highly significant factor was in play here. She was not able to say the words, "I love you," to me. I could tell her, but the moments that would follow were uneasy for both of us. She told me that she felt love, but that she couldn't actually say those three words out loud. In her family, they'd never said 'I love you' when she was a kid, and she didn't know how to now. For me, not hearing those words was just as painful as the sexual dysfunction. What I did not realize at the time was that her inability to say I love you was an overt and external manifestation of my internal reality that I was not loveable. I became depressed. This was the period of time in which I started writing poetry.

"I Know You"

"I know you,"
But what does this mean?
Knowledge must be more
Than merely what is seen.

"But I do know you,
I know your name."
To know means in depth
Just a title is not the same.

"But I do know you,
We've been friends for a long time."
Yes but your experience is yours
And mine is mine.

To know a person
Means more than a name.
A name gives a hint
To his role in the game.

The role in the game
A façade made with care.
That's never let down
So the real person is bare.

To let all be known
Your dreams and your fears
Takes more than acquaintance
Not merely years.

To open your heart
To say this is me.
There's nothing more beautiful
For any man to see.

***

"Escape"

The need to run
A perilous task.
The flight to illusion
The wearing a mask.

The desire for change
To end the disparity.
Can only be solved
By confronting reality.

To change the world
One must be sure
That he doesn't run from void to void
To effect his cure.

Peace with the world
Can only be achieved
When one confronts himself
And satisfaction is justly believed.

My depression and my continued sexual experience led me to enter therapy for the first time. I don't remember how long I remained in treatment, but I do remember that I went as far as I could with that particular therapist. We both had our limitations. Two significant things did come out of that process. One was that I broke up with my girlfriend. The other was that I knew that therapy alone was not going to give me what I wanted and needed for my growth. I was missing an essential spiritual component.

***

Especially In Adversity,
The Faith Of Love Calls Us
To Relate To That Sacred
Unwounded Place That Lies
Within Our Beloved.

Of Course, An Abundance
Of Sex And Danish Won't
Hurt Either.

(My holiday card 2004)

CHAPTER TEN
Marriage: Part I

I was still an undergraduate when I broke up with Natasha. A few months after I'd broken up with her, she started therapy with the same therapist that I'd been seeing. I don't remember the exact time frame, but there came a time when our therapist told me that he thought that she had progressed to the point where I could start dating her again. Despite the fact that I had stopped my therapy, the therapist allowed me to call him to talk about her progress. I contacted her, and to my joy, she consented to see me. I could write a whole other book about what is clinically and ethically wrong about what that therapist did. I was not in a position then to know this, and I doubt that I would have cared. I am in a position to know this now, and boy do I ever care about these things in my life and practice. That therapist should not have seen my girlfriend, and he certainly should not have told me when she was "ready," or anything else about her therapy sessions, for that matter.

We started dating again; much to my utter joy, my penis and I had made friends. Everything worked just fine! I even had a girlfriend who could tell me that she loved me. So, I had all the sex, love, and decent cheese danish I could want in my life. In addition, her apartment was within walking distance to NYU. So I moved in, and all was great.

That heavenly bliss was shattered one night when we were coming back to our apartment, and we were mugged. The apartment was a fifth-floor walk-up. An outside door led into a small vestibule with another interior door. As I was unlocking the inside door, three large guys came in.

"There's a gun pointed at your dick," one of them said.

If I ever go into the robbery business, I will definitely use that line. In just seven words, he had my complete attention and desire to cooperate. He demanded all of our money. I only had $1 on me. My girlfriend had $17. We gave it all to him. We were amazingly lucky because they just turned around and left without hurting us. I simply opened the door, and we started walking up the five flights of stairs. Somewhere around the third floor I heard an ear-piercing scream. Natasha had just come out of her trance and into the reality of what had happened.

When we got into our apartment, we held each other, and I had the following internal monologue: *We can't stay here, because it isn't safe for her. We can't afford any more in rent, so I have to get a job. As long as I have to get a job, I might as well get married.* I didn't think that was a good time to propose, so I waited for the following day. The next day, I started the process of getting a license to teach school. This was the only way I knew of making money while still being able to go to school and stay away from the Vietnam War. In the late sixties, if a young man taught in an area of New York City that was undesirable enough, he received an occupational deferment.

The next day I said, "What would you say if I asked you to marry me?" My bride to be said, "Yes," and three months later, we got hitched. My proposal was not the stuff from which really good romance novels are made. In my defense, later in life I had an opportunity for another proposal, and that's the one that I'd want in the movie. I must admit that, at that time in my life, the decision to get married was quite easy, since, in my mind, I was already in love and committed. I also knew beyond a shadow of doubt that I'd never again convince anyone as pretty or as intelligent as Natasha to say yes.

I have to give my parents credit here. Part of my plan was for us to immediately move in with my parents in Queens because I couldn't yet pay rent. They agreed without hesitation. There we were, sharing a room in a two-bedroom apartment, and we weren't married. This was 1968, and it was by no means the norm of the time. My parents never said a word about the criticism they endured for allowing it. My brother, however, was enraged at both my parents and me for allowing such flagrant immorality. In addition, the girl I was marrying was a *shiksa* (Yiddish for a non-Jew). Again, my parents never said a negative word about that, either.

Then came one of my mother's rare moments. She had an opinion, articulated it, and made it happen! Natasha and I didn't care where we got married. Actually, that probably wasn't true. Since we didn't have a lot of money and my Natasha's parents also didn't have a lot, we hoped for a simple affair. That way any extra money could go towards furniture and other essentials. My mother would have none of that. "Ritchie got married at Leonard's, so you're getting married at Leonard's." For those of you who just happen to not be New York Jews, Leonard's of Great Neck was the quintessential wedding factory for New York and Long Island Jews back then. At any given moment there were probably five or six weddings happening at the same time. What was also cool was that Leonard's allowed an Ethical Culture minister to marry us.

For our wedding I wrote the following vows:

You are my love.
You are my strength
With you I shall grow.
Please be only yourself.

I must admit that, while I thought I understood what those words meant, this was one of those moments that I really didn't have a clue. Before I continue, here is a poem about marriage that I wrote when I was going through my depression at age twenty.

Marriage

The meaning of purpose
An uncertain road,
One traveled by all
Often too heavy a load.

The unbounded dreams
That start to diminish,
Are lost in the world
And crushed to their finish.

They start down that road
Always Spring the season,
Soon turns to Winter
They journey for the wrong reason.

The unvaried routine
Taken by men and their wives,
An unnourished existence
That shatters their lives.

The road has its dangers
Its end reached only by some,
Must be travelled together
Never made by one.

We all have our needs
We all have our dreams,
The mistake often made
It's the end not the means.

The bond is forever
For all the world to see,
Two separate lives
The union of two so that they may be free.

When I wrote these things, I was in no position to understand that, "the union of two so that they may be free" and "please be only yourself" were absolute bulls-eyes. It also never dawned on me that the target was pasted on my forehead. The man who my wife married navigated the world as if he needed to atone for some unknown sin. He was relatively unaware of his own wants and needs. He didn't know that it was okay to be a man. He needed to find someone to fix in order to feel better about himself. His unconscious hope was that if he could find someone that needed fixing, and he succeeded, that would translate into transforming himself into someone worthy of love. Most of this was outside his conscious awareness.

***

I spent the next six years teaching elementary school, getting a doctorate, and just doing whatever else needed to be done. Natasha and I were both in agreement that we did not want to have children yet. It was not a particularly easy or fun-filled period in our lives. It would not have been easy for anyone to be married to me at that time. My day started at 6 a.m. and ended at 11 p.m. On more than one occasion, Natasha asked me, "When are you going to have a life?"

My response was always, "As soon as there are three letters after my name." I don't know how many hundreds of pages Natasha typed for me while I was earning my Ph.D. I was fortunate that she had the ability and was willing to do it.

I was aware of not really being happy in our marriage at that time. I attributed most of my unhappiness to hating my job as a teacher and having to endure the grind of graduate school. I was also vaguely aware of a mutual dissatisfaction with our sex life, and I thought that my primary job was to understand what Natasha thought was wrong and to unilaterally fix it.

***

While living in a small apartment with my parents and Natasha was challenging, it gave me the opportunity to observe from an early adult perspective many of the conditions that had contributed to the creation of my world view. Though it would be years before I was able to understand the relevance of these things, nevertheless I subconsciously filed them away for future reflection. One such observation occurred on Thanksgiving.

Every year, my parents had Thanksgiving at their apartment. The regulars came, and every so often so did a few other guests. The meal was the same each year, and it was actually delicious. Ritchie and I could always count on my mother baking apple pies and, my favorite, her "special cake." I don't know a name for it, but it looked like strudel. Visualize a rugelach on steroids.

Thanksgiving was the opportunity for my father to share our "normal" dinner experience with a wider audience. What this meant was that my father would verbally destroy our guests. I have no idea why anyone would ever return for a second helping of that treat. There was another agenda going on at Thanksgiving that I was not aware of at the time. I later found out that very often one of the guests would be someone with whom my father was having an affair.

Around 1969 or 1970, the guests noticed that I was unusually mellow at dinner. When they inquired why, I casually informed them that I had smoked a joint before eating, and they laughed. The following year, many of them arranged for me to smoke a joint with them so that they could have the same experience. My mother was intrigued, but because she had recently given up smoking cigarettes, she was too afraid to try. The following summer, I suggested that my parents try eating a brownie made with marijuana. We used the occasion of going to Cunningham Park to hear the New York Philharmonic Orchestra as an opportunity to indulge.

I had never baked grass brownies before, so I didn't know the proper recipe. I made a sheet of brownies, and I mixed in an ounce of marijuana—back then grass was $25 an ounce. Before going over to my parents' place, I ate one. I kid you not when I tell you that it did not taste good at all. Natasha suggested that we not tell my mother about the taste, because if we did she wouldn't eat it. When we got to their place, my mother took one bite and said, "I imagine this is what shit tastes like." However, she and my father did each eat one. Natasha and I had another, and I drove the twenty-minute drive to the park. There was an explosion of the use of marijuana in the area in 1971, so I didn't think of the fact that I was sharing grass with my parents as extraordinary. I was, however, shocked that my mother wanted to try it.

Despite whatever differences my now ex-wife and I might still have, I believe that she would agree that what took place next was my greatest achievement with her in her eyes. There were thousands of people in a big field all lying on blankets waiting for the concert to begin. Natasha asked me to accompany her to the bathroom. Somewhere between the blanket and the bathroom, both of us departed the confines of the known universe. To this day she has no idea how I was able to find my parents in that crowd after we left the bathroom. I have no idea what was in that grass, but I am not exaggerating when I tell you that I did not hear the *1812 Overture*. I saw it in brilliant colors. It was wonderful. After the concert, I drove my parents home and us back to our apartment.

The next day I was in a statistics class at NYU, and it dawned on me that I was still stoned. My next thought was *holy shit, my mother.* When I got home, I called my parents. When my mother answered, I tentatively asked her how she liked the night before. I was so relieved when all she said was that she felt relaxed. "However," she added, "your father wants to know how you drove home. He says we spent about twenty minutes waiting at a light on the way back." Of course we hadn't; he was just stoned. I've never had a "bad trip" with any drugs. Despite that, and for no reasons that I want to take personal credit for, I was never into smoking grass a lot. It was fun when I did it, but months or years could go by before I did it again, and I don't remember the last time that I had it.

I have one other grass-related story that I'd like to relate. As I've previously written, my father was an audiophile who built amplifiers for many people. One year, a number of them threw him a thank you party. The group included both family and friends. Yet again my father used that opportunity to trash someone. This time it was one of his sisters. What was just as sad was that her husband was there, and he was joining in with my father. I was probably twenty-four, and even though I was still profoundly out of touch with many things, I was acutely aware of how inappropriate this was and how badly I felt for my aunt. During this same dinner, someone told a joke that I found quite funny. I was sitting next to my father, and I started to laugh. He immediately put his hand on my shoulder and said, "Down boy." I didn't think much of this until Natasha started to chastise my father. I was shocked. I'm not sure I had ever seen anyone chastise my father before. When she said, "Now he can't even laugh?" I smiled, but I'm fairly certain I didn't know what the big deal was about. I appreciated the fact that she stood up for me, but it had never dawned on me to do it for myself. I don't remember any reaction from my father. Nor do I remember talking about the incident with Natasha afterwards.

After my father had finished destroying his sister, one of the non-family members suggested that we go over to his place to smoke some grass, and we all did. I remember sitting on the floor with my back up against a wall and seeing my father walking down the hallway towards me. When he got close, I became overrun with fear. I knew at that moment he was going to "smash my nuts." I immediately curled up to protect myself, and he walked by without incident. I was shocked at both my reaction and the strength of that reaction. Sadly, it would take about another twenty years for me to understand what was happening at that moment. For some reason the marijuana had allowed me to tap into the terror that pervaded my relationship with my father.

It is easier now, in the present, to place events like these into a context that reveals how my childhood experiences molded my worldview. But back then, even as an adult in my twenties, I did not yet have a broad enough understanding to use the things I observed during that time to significantly alter my perception. I have said before that I still view myself as a work in progress. I was also a work in progress then. The difference is that now I know that.

CHAPTER ELEVEN
Teaching School

I taught elementary school from 1968 to 1974. I had never had any intention of becoming a schoolteacher. However, because of what was taking place in my life at that time, it seemed to be an ideal solution for everything I needed.

One of my neighbors just happened to be the principal of an elementary school in the South Bronx. He wrote me a letter stating that I had a teaching position if I could procure a license, so I took that letter down to the Board of Education. This was one of those times where even though I don't have a belief that God intervenes in our lives, something was sure there to help. I arrived at the board with my school transcripts. The board accepted all of my psychology classes as education classes. They then administered an exam, and I walked out a licensed elementary school teacher.

I got my license during May of 1968, and I was going to start teaching third grade in September without ever having taken an education class or having done any student teaching. I had a friend whose mother was a secretary for a junior high in Queens, so I decided to gain some practice by substitute teaching there. I pictured my own experiences in school and my own teachers; that was the only model I had, so with that "expertise" I entered the junior high. This school was not in a great area. I don't remember what subject I was supposed to be teaching. I assure you it didn't matter; I had a lesson plan to follow. I entered the class and attempted to gain some order in the room.

"Excuse me. Would everyone please sit down?" My request fell on deaf ears. I increased my decibel level, but that did nothing. One young girl's behavior was especially unruly, so I went over to her and asked her to please sit down. She ignored me. "If you don't sit down, I'm taking you to the principal's office!"

She instantly turned towards me, and from a few inches away she said, "Who gives a shit about the fucking principal?" I spent the rest of the day and the next just hoping no one got killed on my watch. Thankfully, a few kind students took me under their wings.

So with all of my educational training, I walked into P.S. 49 in the South Bronx of New York City in September 1968. Despite everything that I have just written, if you could have listened to what was going on in my head at that moment, you would have heard the words to the song "To Sir with Love." However, though I was as hopeful as Sidney Poitier's character had been, I was neither as successful nor as good-looking.

For the first two years, I taught third grade. I hated every moment of it. Every day I experienced myself as an utter failure. I had thirty-two kids, and I wasn't doing a very good job of teaching them what they needed to learn. That year, I was physically ill more than at any other time in my life. I'm sure part of this was due to the fact that these darlings carried numerous diseases unknown to medical science. The other part was due to my level of stress.

The custom in elementary school was to write "the heading" on the board in the front of the room:

P.S. 49
September 10, 1968
Mr. Sherman
Class 3-205

Starting with my second year of teaching, I added something to my heading on the upper left corner of the board. On the first day of school, that addition looked like this: 188/10. Three days went by before one of my students asked me what it meant. I told him that the 188 was the number of days left in the school year. The ten was the number of sick days that I had left. My first year I had exceeded my allotted ten days.

I tried really hard to do a good job. The kids in my class were clearly bright. I just couldn't find a way to tap into that intelligence within the confines of those walls and consistently produce great results. However, when I had the opportunity to work one-on-one with a student, I felt somewhat successful. I was able to take the time to answer questions and phrase things in a way that allowed for better understanding. I also believe that experiencing the full attention of the teacher allowed individual students to focus better and to feel worthy of someone's time.

One day during my first year, the door to my classroom opened without warning and in walked a very large Hispanic woman. She walked up to my desk and informed me that she was "Sammy's" mother.

"How is he doing?" she asked.

Sammy was one of my bigger problems. I didn't know how to tell her that he was a major pain in my ass, but then I had a stroke of genius.

"How's Sammy doing at home?" I asked.

For years I have told my clients that only shrinks and Jews are allowed to answer questions with questions. I was a teacher before I was a shrink, so I guess that was the Jew in me talking.

"Ugh, I want to kill him," she said.

I laughed and gave the mother a look of acknowledgement. "That's exactly how I feel," I said.

She jerked him out of his seat and dragged him to the front of the class, where she began whipping him with her belt. I stopped her as quickly as I could, and fortunately she left my class. I probably was the most shaken up one in the room. The kids reacted as if what they had just witnessed was business as usual, but I was shocked. My father had never whipped me. The only physical punishments he doled out were spankings. But I did live in terror of my father. Perhaps witnessing that whipping unconsciously put me in touch with what I feared was always beneath the surface with him.

Back in the sixties, there were no controversies about teachers sexually abusing their students, so nobody flinched when I started taking some of my students to my apartment on weekends. Natasha and I enjoyed taking them to the movies or on picnics. One of the first students whom I took home was Jaycee. Jaycee was a thin, very dark-skinned boy who always had a scowl on his face. He appeared constantly angry. My school was located in the Mott Haven section of the South Bronx, a place I wouldn't walk at night when I first got there. This part of New York City had the highest arson rate in the world. Teachers frequently came out of school to find their cars up on boxes because their tires had been stolen.

I drove to pick up Jaycee to take him out for dinner on a Friday after school. His apartment building had a broken window in the lobby, and the stairs smelled of urine. As I knocked on the front door, I could hear a baby crying. I was not prepared for what I saw when the door opened. Jaycee's mother greeted me with a smile, and I could see that one bulb hanging from a cord lit the main room. The apartment was staggeringly dark and filled with too many kids and too much noise. At that instant I began to realize exactly what I was up against in my efforts to teach. How could I possibly expect Jaycee to be able to do his work and not look anything but angry? This awareness did allow me to have more compassion for my students. Unfortunately, this compassion did not translate into any less stress for me.

The current political rhetoric from those who claim to have "religious authority" in America would like us to believe that the Socialist Liberals, as represented by President Obama, would like to threaten the "wonderful opportunities" that "we" Americans have. They characterize the poor as basically only interested in welfare. They assure us all that if those on welfare only had the proper work ethic they could easily fulfill the American dream. This is such a total crock of shit. I'd love for all of them to be forced to live in Jaycee's apartment for the eight years that he was there.

I took Jaycee back home after dinner, and the next day I picked him up again and took him to the movies. The movie that he selected was *2001: A Space Odyssey*. I had already seen the movie, and I was not at all sure how he'd react because there were a few things in the movie that I didn't understand. He watched the entire movie in total awe. When it was over, he had a wonderful smile on his face and he had no difficulties in sharing with me his understanding about what it all meant.

Most of my students had a great deal of intelligence. They were living in a war zone, and they had more street smarts than all of Congress combined. None of them was there by choice. I can't imagine how many thousands of Jaycees will never be in a position to realize their potential and make use of their superior capacities. The ghettos of America have the potential of producing far more than great athletes and rap artists.

***

"Whatever you did for one of the least of these brothers and sisters of mine, you did for me."
—Matthew 25:31-46

CHAPTER TWELVE
The Gift of Rejection

Sometime during 1970 Arthur Janov published *The Primal Scream*. I read this book and I was impressed. Later that year I saw his presentation about his new Primal Scream therapy, and it somehow made sense to me. After I read his next book, *The Anatomy of Mental Illness*, I decided that I wanted to become a Primal Therapist. I applied to the training center and was granted an admissions interview.

Natasha and I flew to Los Angeles. She had a cousin who was married to a Mexican man, and we had fun with their family. I was introduced to mescal and somehow found myself eating the worm that's in the bottle. I also learned that with sufficient mescal, the hot chilies in the food no longer burned my throat. While I didn't get drunk, for some reason the following morning when Natasha opened the blinds to our motel room I felt like someone was trying to burn out my eyeballs.

I went to the Primal Scream Center in Beverly Hills for what proved to be the most bizarre interview of my life. Janov's wife, who was the head of training, handled the questioning, and after learning the requisite information about my education and experience, she asked me why I wanted to be a Primal Therapist. She asked me why I thought that I needed Primal Therapy. I told her about which of my issues I though would benefit from Priamal Therapy.

"Also," I said, "if I'm going to be a Primal Therapist, I'd like to have first-hand knowledge of the process."

"We have thousands of applicants," she said. "Why should we give this opportunity to you?"

"As I said," I told her, "my particular issues would benefit from…"

But she was already shaking her head.

"Well, my primary intention is to be trained as a therapist anyway," I said.

"That's still not enough," she said. "Why should we pick you over the thousands of others."

This is when things got bizarre. I found myself trying to convince this woman that I was sick enough to warrant their precious therapy. I had not yet learned to trust my gut and get my ass out of this surreal set of circumstances. I left there still hoping to win the prize of being damaged enough for them to want me but convinced that I would not be chosen. Sure enough, a couple of weeks later I got a letter denying my application.

This was the first time in my life that I felt the sting of rejection in regards to my training and or intellect. Despite the fact that the interview was bizarre, the rejection bummed me out.

At that time, the principal of the school where I was teaching had given me a most wonderful gift. The school had found money in the budget to employ a second guidance counselor, so my days of torture in the classroom were over for one year. Oddly enough, a student intern guidance counselor in our school had recently applied to the Primal Institute and had been accepted! She took a leave of absence from the school and went out to Los Angeles. About one month later, she was back at work.

Apparently the institute was only interested in totally compliant people who would not ask questions or make waves. My colleague could not tolerate such an environment, and so she dropped out. All of a sudden what had happened to me took on a whole new look. I was filled with gratitude that I had not paid the expense to find this out on my own. I had received a lesson in faith and humility, and I got a glimpse at the possibility that—perhaps in the long run—things work out for the best. I vowed to temper my arrogance and certitude in the future. After all, I don't always know what the right ending to the movie ought to be.

CHAPTER THIRTEEN
The Trip

In 1974, when it became clear that I was finally going to get my doctorate, Natasha suggested that we go away for four months. I had already taken a leave of absence from my school job to complete my doctorate, and she was also able to take a leave of absence from her job. We gave up our apartment and put our belongings in storage. Natasha had been learning about Zen Buddhism and said that she'd like to go to India. India has nothing to do with Zen, but I didn't care. I loved the idea of going away, and on my own I probably wouldn't have picked India. As a result, she was ultimately the one who was responsible for me meeting my spiritual teacher.

Our pending trip also prompted my parents to give me the best material gift that I ever received from them. After I got my doctorate, they gave me a Pentax Spotmatic 35mm camera. It was a wonderful camera for its day and my first 35mm. The 35mm format SLR (single lens reflex) allows for interchangeable lenses. I immediately went downtown and bought some lenses.

The gift was a total shock. My father and I never really talked about photography, so I have no idea what prompted that decision. When I was a teenager, my father showed me how to develop film. We never discussed if either of us had an approach to photography. We never discussed composition. I never heard my father say anything about my shots. This absence of dialogue was another aspect of my "normal."

I had no time between when I got the camera and when we left for our trip for me to get acquainted with it. While we were away, I would mail my parents ten rolls of exposed film or slides at a time to be developed. In 1974 one did not want to have 35mm film processed in India. During our trip—which turned out to be a lot longer than just four months—we lived in Tehran for a while. This allowed time for my parents to develop some shots and mail them back to me.

I have no idea if I would have ever pursued photography if we had never taken that trip and if my parents had not given me that camera. What is also fascinating is that, despite the fact that I was not able to see my images, they improved over time.

I had secured us student tickets to sail from New York to London on the QE 2. Those tickets cost $200 each. You see, there were some advantages to living in the Middle Ages. Our plan was to spend some time in England and then fly to Thailand. From Thailand we would fly to Calcutta and then take the next three months to go overland from Calcutta to Brussels. We had a return flight from Brussels to New York booked, so all was set.

We left New York on April 15, 1974. I had never been on a cruise ship or on the ocean before. The next day we were standing on the rear of the ship, and I was staring out at an infinity of water and sky. I turned to Natasha and said that I would like us to cash in our return tickets from Brussels. I didn't want the pressure of having to be in Belgium at a certain time and I wanted to consider playing the trip totally by ear. After all, we could purchase the return tickets anytime we wanted. Amazingly, she agreed. I had resolved that this trip would be a spiritual quest. I had no idea what I would find or where I would find it, but I wanted to be open to taking whatever opportunities availed themselves.

As a teenager, I was attracted to reading about Eastern approaches to spirituality. The science fiction of Frank Herbert and Arthur C. Clarke resonated within me. Alan Watts, Ram Dass, and Aldous Huxley were some of my favorite authors. These writers gave me the sense that eventually I'd find some practice or approach that would provide me with a context for my spiritual longing.

However magical cruising on a luxury liner was, it did not really help to decrease the sense of distance that I felt from Natasha. That distance made sense to me in light of how intense the previous six years had been, and I was hoping that all the time we were about to spend together would allow us to establish a greater sense of closeness. I was wrong.

Thailand was fun. But all through our adventures there we kept hearing about trouble in India. For the first time in the history of the country there was going to be a train strike. Many "expert" world travelers—think hippy, no money, questionable hygiene practices—warned us that we were making a mistake in going to India. Nevertheless we took the risk of flying from Bangkok to Calcutta. On the bus to the airport Natasha said, "Maybe if we're lucky the plane will crash," and we both laughed.

Nothing in my previous twenty-eight years had prepared me for India. We arrived in Calcutta in May of 1974. I've been back to India at least eleven other times, and I can assure you that you don't want to be in most of Northern India—aside from the Himalayas—in May. As long as global warming doesn't screw things up too much more, India is a place where one pretty much knows what the weather will be if one bothers to check. We hadn't bothered to check, and every day was at least ninety-five degrees. The humidity was in the you've-got-to-be-kidding range. On top of that, add the reality that within Indian culture the sense of personal space is much different than it is in the U.S. As a New Yorker I was accustomed to walking down 5th Avenue surrounded by thousands of people, but rarely did people speak to me. In India everybody talks to you. The most frequently asked question was, "What is the purpose of your journey?" This would be followed by, "What are your qualifications?" The question means, "How far did you get in school?" After that, people often asked,

"Were you a virgin when you got married?" I assure you there were many more questions and, at that time, about six hundred million people ready to ask them. The food was too spicy. The dirt in the air was suffocating. The poverty was staggering. The variations and manifestations of deformity were more staggering. I felt I was always one bite of food away from amoebic dysentery. Nothing worked. Getting from one place to another not only required an act of God, it also took three times longer than I estimated. By the time we had been in India about four weeks, I'd have gladly given the border guard all of my money if that's what it would have taken to get into Pakistan.

When I was on the stern of the *QE 2*, I had realized that I'd wanted this trip to be a spiritual journey. I only had a sense that I wanted to learn how to have a direct experience of the divine. I had no idea what form it would take, and it didn't really matter to me. What mattered was that I wanted to *feel* a sense of connection. I wanted more than a belief system. Since I had no idea where to look, I was hoping that along the way I would find a teacher who would show me. Before we went to India I assumed that if I was lucky I would find one there. However, by the time we left India, I knew that I'd never find anything but aggravation there. Yet again I was wrong.

I took the image on page 112, "Wake Up Call," in Varanasi, India, during May 1974. Varanasi is the holiest city in India. It is the place where all Hindus would like to be cremated and have their ashes thrown into the Ganges River. I have since returned to Varanasi at least ten more times. It is the place where I feel the closest to God.

The man in the shot is a little person. The left side of his body is pretty much non-functional. His left eye is oozing. His left leg is permanently bent in that position. The white between his legs is the rice that he will eat that day. There is a walking stick on his right that he uses to hop around. Three hours after I took that shot, I could not walk on the rock he had been sitting on, because it was so hot. He was not there when I returned in 1975. I assumed that he was dead.

I have this shot hanging in my office as well as in my bathroom at home. He is what I see everyday when I get out of the shower. When I am conscious enough to look, he serves as a powerful reminder to me that whatever I think are my problems, I ain't got shit.

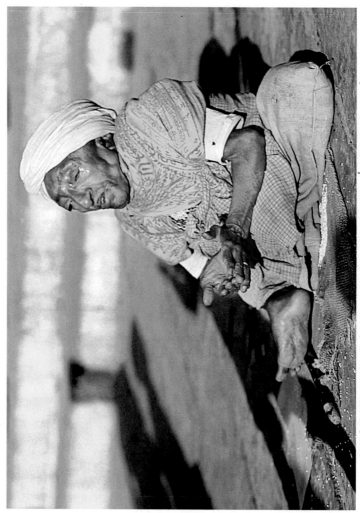

WAKE UP CALL - VARANASI, INDIA, 5/74

CHAPTER FOURTEEN
The Trip Continues

When we left India, we traveled overland to the west to Pakistan. We had a pretty much uneventful experience there. In those days, one could go to the American Embassy in Islamabad—I think it was on Thursday nights—to see a movie and have some alcohol. Little did we know that we were so close to where Osama bin Laden would eventually be killed. We didn't even know about Osama bin Laden.

Peshawar (pronounced Pe-shower) is the closest city to the border with Afghanistan. It was famous for its "thieves market." Peshawar has always been a great place to purchase illegal goods of any kind. One afternoon while we were there, we went to a restaurant. Two Western women were sitting in the garden having lunch. In those days Pakistan was not a place for single Western women, so I couldn't resist asking them why they were there. They informed me that they were on a holiday. When they found out that we were leaving to go to Kabul, Afghanistan, they told us that they lived there and that we "had to" come to a party they were having the following Friday.

In 1974, being in Pakistan was like being in the early 1800s, but Kabul, Afghanistan, was more like the 1600s. All the world travelers hung out on Chicken Street. Upon our arrival, we checked in to the Super Pyam Hotel. Our "concierge" was named Esock. (I can't remember what I had for breakfast today, yet I can tell you this!) I had many wonderful days in Afghanistan.

The following Friday we did go to that party. I was unprepared for what awaited us. Here I was, the hot shot Dr. Robert Sherman, and I felt like the most uneducated man in the room. The guests were either relatives of the royal family or the offspring of Afghan diplomats. They spoke perfect English, and many of them had no accent. They had attended schools in Moscow, Paris, and London at places that I couldn't get into if my life depended on it. It was great fun. One of the women whom we'd met in Peshawar had a boyfriend named Sedique. Sedique had a wonderfully deep voice and an accent that made English sound melodic. During the party, Sedique turned to me and said, "Tomorrow, you and your wife are coming with me to Malique's wedding."

"How can you invite us without asking him. And won't they need to prepare extra food?"

When Sedique finally stopped laughing, all he said was, "Anyone who is a friend of mine is a friend of Malique."

Six months later when we were living in Tehran, we learned that if we had people over for dinner, we had to cook for twice as many people as we'd invited. Everywhere from India to Turkey we experienced a most amazing friendliness and hospitality.

One evening we went out to dinner with Sedique. He took us to one of his favorite restaurants in an older part of the city. We were seated at the only table, and it happened to be outside. My wife remained seated while Sedique took me around back where he spoke with the owner in Farsi. These were the days before I could understand Farsi. We happened to be standing next to a few goats. I thought nothing of this because in that part of the world it was common to be in the presence of animals. We went back to the table and sat for what was a fairly long time. Then Sedique turned to me and told me that because I was the guest of honor, I would now have an Afghan delicacy. The server placed a plate in front of me that had two egg-shaped objects on it. It would have been quite disrespectful for me to decline the honor, so I proceeded to eat one of those darling goat gonads. Then I realized that we had been waiting this long because they had slaughtered and cooked one of those goats. The meal was actually quite good, and for better or worse, perhaps that goat has contributed something that has made me or my sons the men we are today.

***

Natasha and I realized that we were going to have to find a way to make some money because we wanted to extend our trip, but we had only brought enough with us for a four-month journey. There was a huge U.S. Aid base in Kabul, with about 1800 families in residence. I learned that the base was looking for a psychologist, so I applied for the position. I passed the first interview, and then the head of personnel for the American Embassy interviewed me. That interview went well, and he told me that as far as he was concerned, I had the job, but first it would have to be approved in Washington. He implied that I might not get the job, because he may be required to hire from stateside. Indeed he was required to hire someone from the U.S. I wonder what would have happened to the rest of our lives if we had stayed there and lived in Kabul. I know that, at least in the beginning, I would have loved it. I really liked Afghanistan and the Afghan people. I found them to be fierce, proud, respectful, and I had a sense that I could have learned much from being there.

During the process, I met a man who was the Pakistani Air Attaché, and he invited Natasha and me to dinner at his home. That dinner was one of the most bizarre in my life. It was only him and his wife and us.

Very soon after dinner began, he turned to me and said, "You know, my wife and I don't love each other."

I quickly looked at his wife to see if she was holding any cutlery. She didn't look fazed at all.

"We don't have the same illusion of romantic love that you do in the West," he continued. "Of course, we respect each other and perhaps in time we will also come to love each other."

"You don't mind that you didn't get to choose your wife?" I asked.

"Not at all," he said. "Our parents know us very well, and they had very good reasons for the choices that they made. You know, we also do not have the same problem of so many divorces as you do in your country."

His wife neither said a word nor gave any indication of disagreement or anger. My guess is that Gloria Steinem's work was not popular in Pakistan.

When we left Kabul, we took a bus to Herat, the town closest to the Iranian border. We had dinner at our hotel and noticed some French tourists who had a short wave radio. We sat there and listened to Richard Nixon's resignation speech.

We had heard that it was possible to get work teaching English in Tehran, so that was our plan. In 1974, parts of Tehran looked like a European city. Several main streets had two lanes in each direction and plenty of traffic. I had the sense that the Shah was pouring a tremendous amount of money into the infrastructure of the country and that many of the people could not keep up with the rapid changes. People would wander across busy streets without looking at the cars. They almost looked like they were crossing a dirt road in a village where the worst that could happen is that some donkey might bump into them.

The first day we went looking for work, we found jobs teaching English at the Iran America Society. Incidentally, this was one of the places where hostages were taken in 1979 during what became known as the Iran hostage crisis. When we were there in 1974, however, we were in absolutely no danger. On the first day of teaching, we were told that all of our mail and phone conversations would be monitored. We were also told to never discuss sex, politics, or religion in our classes. As long as we followed these rules, we would avoid any trouble.

The taxis in Tehran stop running at midnight. Very often we were at a party and needed a ride home at two a.m., so we did exactly what the Persians would do. We stood on the street and waited for a car to drive by. If the driver was interested in making some money, he would slow down and ask where we were going. We then paid him what would have been the taxi fare. Just imagine getting in to a stranger's car in Tehran nowadays!

We stayed in Tehran for ten months. During that time, we were able to earn more than $1800 per month teaching English for four hours a day, four days per week. We lived a sumptuous lifestyle that included a lot of sightseeing, shopping, and eating out. Those were the days when Americans in the U.S. were enduring gas rationing and had to get their ten gallons of gas on odd or even days. (A person's license plate number determined his or her day.) If we had stayed longer, we could have renegotiated our contracts and made even more money. We had just one slight problem. Natasha was molested on a regular basis! The second day we were there, she started wearing a chador, the long scarf that Persian women wear over their heads. It does not cover their faces as the burqa does in Afghanistan. The chador didn't help a whole lot. What made things more difficult for me was that she insisted I promise her that, no matter what happened, I would not assault any of the men. She was concerned that I would wind up in jail. So we were both rather tense whenever we would walk the streets. On a number of occasions, some guy would touch her in an inappropriate way. One time we were walking on the street that leads to the bazaar in the poorer section of Tehran. We went there because that was the location of my favorite rug shop. All of a sudden Natasha broke into a run back up the way we had just come. Once I realized what was happening, I ran as quickly as I could to catch her. By the time I reached her, she was hitting a man. I pulled her off of him, and she said, "But he's not dead yet."

I certainly didn't blame her for her reaction. It appeared that the relatively uneducated men there viewed Western women as whores based on what they'd seen in Western movies. The well-educated upper-class men, however, had wives who flew to Paris to have their nails done, so their public behavior was quite different.

We had estimated that we'd need $10,000 for the rest of our trip. The moment we had it, we left the country.

During one of our sightseeing trips in Iran, we went to Shiraz. Shiraz is one of the holiest cities in the country. While we were there, we saw a most interesting man. He appeared to be quite old—I later found out he was ninety-three—and he was dressed in an unusual way. He approached us and in Farsi asked if he could take our picture. After he did, we spoke to him for a while, and when he found out that we were living in Tehran, he invited us to his place. By that time we had taken some Farsi classes so we could speak enough to get around. A few weeks later we went over to his place with a friend who spoke much better Farsi then we did.

While we were at his apartment, we learned that he was a Sufi. Sufis are the mystical sect of Islam. At 11 p.m. he insisted on making us some rice to eat. While the rice was cooking, he placed a cigar box full of money in front of us. He said that if we needed any money, we should feel free to take some. If we had any extra we could also feel free to give him some. We asked him what the money was for. He told us that it would pay for his funeral.

What a wonderful opportunity. Here I am on my spiritual journey, and I am face to face with a mystic.

"Hajji, what do you think will happen when you die?" I asked.

He looked me straight in the eyes and shared the wisdom of his ninety-three years. "How the hell should I know?" he said. While we were there, he gave me a ring. The ring has an amber colored stone with Arabic script on it. The script has been translated for me as, "Property of God." He told me that as long as I wore the ring, my enemies could not hurt me. I have worn the ring ever since, and so far he seems to have been correct.

***

After we left Iran, we traveled through Turkey and then on to Greece where we spent four glorious weeks on a small island. In Greece we hitchhiked on a truck. It was the only time we had ever hitched. While on the truck, we reached a point where we had to make a decision as to what we were going to do over the next few days. Our choices were to stay in Greece, go to Israel, or head back to India. How amazing it was to have those choices. We decided to return to India.

We spent the next few months traveling overland through Turkey, Iran, Afghanistan, and Pakistan to India. When we were in Kabul, I had purchased a lot of carpets and other woven goods. I then bought a tin trunk to ship the stuff home. A shipping agent in Kabul told me it would be much easier for me to ship it from Pakistan. I hired two guys to carry the trunk to the bus station, where I witnessed one of the most amazing things that I have ever seen. The large trunk needed to be placed on top of the bus. One of the men picked up the trunk and put it on his head. He then climbed a set of stairs on the back of the bus and put the trunk on the roof. The trunk weighed 440 pounds.

Crossing the border from Iran to Afghanistan (near Mashhad, Iran) was fascinating. The Iranian side looked pretty much like you would expect. The Afghan side looked kind of like a Boy Scout shack. The officers all wore different uniforms with torn fabric. Some had guns and some did not. Most of the guns did not have bullets. I found this out simply by asking the officers. The first time we had gone through, one of the guards invited us to have tea in the back. I guess these guys saw two non-hippies and were interested in where we had been and why we were traveling. Plus it happened to be a slow day at the border.

We sat there having our tea and saw a pile of passports of people who were waiting to cross. The guards laughed as they looked at the pictures. There was clearly no urgency of any kind to do anything.

Incidentally, when we were in the waiting area the second time at the border, we knew not to expect anything to happen quickly. The border was unusually busy the day we arrived, and so many people were waiting and nothing was happening. We waited in a small room that had mud walls and a mud floor and was lined with wooden benches. A radio played music in another room where the guards stayed. As we waited, a tour bus arrived and a lot of people got out. The tour leader gave one of the guards all the passports from the group and most likely some *baksheesh* (bribe money). The guards glanced at the passports while we remained waiting. Suddenly, a middle-aged American woman who had also been waiting stood up and started yelling at the Afghan guard. She told him in no uncertain terms that she had been waiting a long time and that these people had come after her, and as an American she was not going to tolerate seeing them be processed ahead of her. The officer did not flinch. He asked the lady for her name. He went in the back and retrieved her passport. He then handed it to her.

"This is my border and you will not be crossing it today."

"Please, sir, I am sorry. Of course, you can do whatever you like. Please let me pass into Pakistan."

I laughed as I watched this "great American powerhouse" melt before our eyes. The woman was still there when we left. She may still be there for all I know. Her behavior would have been inappropriate in any setting, but in this one it was unbelievably stupid.

Natasha and I knew that as Westerners, whether we liked or approved of Afghan culture, we were guests in their country. My experience in Afghanistan was that one needed to learn how to play by the rules. If one did so with respect, that respect was returned even more. If one did not play by the rules, one could get dead.

Now back to the trunk. When we got to Peshawar, I went to a shipping company. An employee told me that I'd been given bad advice. He told me that in order to ship my stuff from Pakistan, I would have to get an export license. Such a thing would be very expensive, and it would take at least two weeks. The shipping agent suggested that I take the trunk back to the border and leave it there in "no man's land." That way his truck could pick up the trunk without an export license because technically it wasn't being shipped from Pakistan. So the next day we hired a taxi to take us—and our trunk—back to the border.

The shipping company man was there, and he had me write a letter beseeching the highest-ranking official at the border to allow me to leave my trunk there. As I was leaving the official's office, I overheard him say to the shipping guy, "What's in this for me?" At that moment I kissed that trunk goodbye. I was wrong. The trunk arrived home without anything missing! But that's not the end of my story.

We left the border and got back into our taxi for the ride back to Peshawar. The route from the border goes through one of the most famous places in world history: the Khyber Pass. Up until bin Laden was killed, it had been rumored that he was living there. The Khyber Pass is technically a part of Pakistan. But even then that was only a technicality. Various tribal leaders or warlords, not the Pakistani government, ruled that region.

It would take far too long to describe what it felt like to place our lives in the hands of drivers in India and Pakistan. Under the best of circumstances, even on roads where there is no traffic, I sensed that catastrophe could be just around the corner.

My experience as a passenger traveling on mountain roads can only be described as a wonderful opportunity to need to feel close to God, because it was only a matter of seconds before I was going to die. Anyway, Natasha and I were in the taxi traveling through the Khyber Pass heading from the border to Peshawar, and all of a sudden our driver began to look very anxious. He was obviously sweating. In addition, he began talking to himself out loud in Urdu, and he kept looking backwards. When I turned around to see what he was looking at, I saw a rapidly approaching car with four men in it. Two of the men were hanging out the sides of the car with drawn guns. The car overtook us and forced us to stop. Two men rushed to our car and dragged our driver to the side of their car and started to beat him up. Natasha and I remained in the back of the cab. We were unable to help our driver, because we were unarmed and I had no idea what was happening and what the correct course of action might be. Then one of the men came over to my side of the cab and spoke to me. As he did so he was playing with the cylinder of his gun. This was a very convincing tactic. He then asked, "Where you get taxi?"

I didn't know the "right" answer to this question, so I said nothing. Meanwhile the other guys continued to make an impression on our driver. The man repeated his question, and I again said nothing.

This time our driver shouted, "Tell him!" I explained that I had hired the taxi in Peshawar to take us to the border, and he was now bringing us back to Peshawar. The man asked me if I was sure that I had not hired the taxi at the border. When I repeated the same story, the man went back to the other men and told them what I had said. They gave our driver one more punch for good luck and let him go. My best guess as to what happened was that the men thought we had just come from Afghanistan and had hired the taxi at the border. If this was true, then our driver had cut the line in front of their taxi, and he would be put out of business on the spot. The rest of the ride back to Peshawar was rather quiet and uneventful.

During the course of my life, I have been fortunate to travel. Aside from having the opportunity to see amazing things, I have also been exposed to diverse ways of living. These experiences have deeply influenced my perspective on life and myself. Total strangers have offered me incredible hospitality. At the beginning of our long stay in Asia, we found ourselves in a hut on stilts in Northern Thailand outside of Chiang Mai. An elderly man offered us the only thing that he had to give, which was a glass of water. This presented us with a significant dilemma: turn down the water and insult the man or drink it and risk amoebic dysentery. We drank the water and fortunately suffered no ill effects. When I see teenagers here driving BMWs to school, I think of the hundreds of children whom I have seen playing with sticks, and I can still hear their whole-body laughter. We have so much to learn about what is really important from sources other than Neiman Marcus catalogs.

CHAPTER FIFTEEN
The Yoga Institute

After we had left Afghanistan the first time and started working in Iran, my wife had begun researching about meditation courses and other things available in India, where we were traveling next. She had heard of a man named Goenka (Satya Narayan Goenka) who taught Vipassana meditation in English once per year. She was under the impression that his class was to start somewhere in India around the middle of September, so we had arranged our schedule to be in India at that time. Because I had had such a horrendous experience in India the first time, I was fairly certain that I was going to want to get out of India as quickly as possible and get to Japan where I would find my teacher. Once again I was wrong.

When we arrived in Amritsar, India, something quite unexpected happened. All the things that had royally pissed me off about India were still there. But, for reasons still unknown to me today, they no longer were a problem for me. I have no idea what had internally shifted during the preceding fourteen months that had resulted in my changed reaction. All I can report is that India had gone from a living hell to become my spiritual home. It's my favorite place to take pictures, and I've since returned many, many times.

In Amritsar, we went to the Golden Temple (Harmandir Sahib) of the Sikhs. The Sikhs are the guys who wear turbans and have long beards. A traditional Sikh never cuts his hair, and he wears a silver bracelet and carries a knife. The Sikhs are considered to have originated from the warrior caste. They are known to be good businessmen in India. I took the picture on page 136, "Golden Temple," at Hermandir Sahib.

From previous travels we had learned to use something called *Poste Restante*. Poste Restante is a wonderful way to receive mail anywhere in the world, though I'm not sure about the States. Once we knew our itinerary, we'd tell our friends to send us mail to the main post office in the nearest city and address the envelope to us in care of Poste Restante. The post office would then hold the mail until we picked it up. When we picked up our mail in Amritsar, we found out that the meditation course had been cancelled. I suggested we go to Nepal because I wanted to go trekking there. Natasha had told our friends to send mail to Bombay, so she wanted us to go there to get our mail. Since I was the captain of the ship and the master of our domain, we went to Bombay.

All throughout our travels, Natasha and I had heard of a place called the Yoga Institute. I knew nothing accurate about yoga, so I was certainly interested in finding out more about it. We were under the impression that we would be able to live and study there, so the day after we picked up our mail in Bombay, we took the Suburban Railroad out to Santa Cruz and found our way to the entrance of the Yoga Institute. From outside the gate we saw a pasty-faced, thin, white male leaving the building in front of us. We called to him, and he came over to the gate. Pasty Face Peter spoke with an Australian accent, and when we told him that we wanted to get some information about staying there, he told us to talk to Dr. Jayadeva. He told us that Dr. Jayadeva's office was in the building in front of us, and we walked in. That moment was the beginning of the rest of my life.

After a relatively short wait, Dr. Jayadeva came in and sat down.

"Hello, can I help you?"

Many Indians speak English, but they do so with a fascinating accent that makes it almost impossible for someone new to India to understand. In my experience, it is best to stare at their mouths and try to convince yourself that you can lip read.

"My name is Bob and this is my wife, Natasha. We are from America, and we would like some information about the possibility of staying at The Yoga Institute"

"Are you yoga teachers in America?"

"No, sir. We don't know very much about yoga, and we would like to learn."

"I think it is best that you take our twenty-one day better living course. You might find that helpful. The class meets for one hour a day."

"Can we stay here?"

"No, I'm sorry only students in our teacher training course can stay here. Here are the names of some hotels in the area that you can stay in."

We left and headed for the first hotel. I was frustrated. I did not want to live in a hotel and "study" yoga for one hour a day. After walking around Santa Cruz for about forty-five minutes, we went back to the office to talk to Dr. Jayadeva again.

During our first talk, Dr. Jayadeva had sat behind a rounded counter top and made no eye contact with me. He spent the entire conversation staring over my right shoulder and out the window behind me. So this time I wanted our interaction to be different. I pulled a chair up to the counter and waited. Again Dr. Jayadeva did not keep us waiting very long. He looked surprised to see us so soon again and asked why we were back. I leaned over the counter to get as close to him as I could.

"We very much appreciate your offer of letting us take the twenty-one day course, but I would like for you to please reconsider your decision and let us stay here. I have within me an ache that I believe is my soul's yearning to be back with God. I am looking for a direction. I don't know if yoga will be my path. All I know is that if you give us the chance, I will use every second that I am here to learn and experience all that you can teach me."

"If you stay, you will have to take two twenty-one day classes a day, one in the morning and one in the evening. In addition, you will also have to take the teacher training classes."

"Of course. We will do whatever you want."

So with that interaction we had just signed ourselves up for Yoga 101, 102 and who knew what else. A couple of days later we moved into The Institute, and low and behold, Pasty Face Peter was my roommate. Men and women did not live together at The Institute. I must admit, at that time, the thought of a three-week separation was fine with me.

Much to my disappointment, our trip and increased time together had not resulted in an increased sense of love and intimacy for me. I thought that I knew how I would like it to be with us. I was aware of some of my hurt and anger about the situation. But we were still operating under the assumption that it was up to me to make things better. If things were going to improve, it would be because I had learned to change my wants and needs.

***

The following morning, Peter asked me if I was interested in doing "Karma Yoga." I asked him what that was, and he told me that it entailed doing some kind of service work for The Institute. When I said yes, we went back in to Dr. Jayadeva's office. Peter told Doctor (this is how I will refer to him from now on) that I wanted to do some Karma Yoga, and

Doctor told him to take me to the roof of the *Bhavan* to clean out the drains. I didn't know why Peter chuckled, but I did notice that for the first time Doctor briefly looked at me.

The *Bhavan* was a large meeting hall where presentations are given to the public and people do their yoga practices. Peter showed me the roof, and my yoga career was off to a flying start. For two days I cleaned animal and bird droppings out of the drains. After I completed that, I went back to Doctor, and he had me wash stairs. After that, he stuck me in a dusty attic that was not big enough for me to be able to stand erect in to clean, sort, and catalog approximately thirty years of journals. As you can readily see, yoga can be a lot of fun. Because I was constantly immersed in dusty environments, I developed a bad sinus infection. I would remain ill with various maladies for the next ten months.

When Natasha learned about my experiences with Karma Yoga, she went to Doctor and asked him for something to do. He told her that she needed her rest, and the best thing she could do was to go to her room and relax. It was probably more difficult for Natasha to relax than it was for me to get up close and personal with bird shit.

In addition to Karma Yoga, we did do both twenty-one day classes and the teacher training classes as Doctor had requested. There were about ten Westerners living at the Institute, all from Europe and Scandinavia. They were serious yoga practitioners and were seeking their yoga teacher certifications. The students were preparing for the arrival of a group from Europe that was going to take a special five-day retreat at The Institute. Within our first week there, Doctor had me preparing study materials for the group. Each day, he would give me a topic, and it was my job to write and print a handout on that topic. That meant I had to go to The Institute's library and research the subject. After that, I typed it on what was probably the world's first typewriter, and I then printed it on the world's first mimeograph machine. All of this was in addition to the classes and other "Karma Yoga" gifts that Doctor bestowed upon me.

This went on for three weeks. At the end of the three weeks, both Natasha and I knew that we wanted to take the full teacher training course. Dr. Jayadeva was a perceptive, intelligent and amazingly calm man, and I knew that he had a lot to teach me. I had reached a turning point in my practice. Performing the *asanas* (poses) no longer made me feel as stiff and inadequate, and I wanted to learn the benefits of continuing. We debated leaving The Institute for a short vacation, but we decided that as long as we were there, we would just keep on going. But we needed Doctor's permission to do this.

So once again we found ourselves in his office having yet another interesting interaction.

"We'd like to stay on and take the teacher training," I said.

"Why?" he asked. "You don't want to be yoga teachers. You won't like it here in the summer. It gets quite humid and uncomfortable."

"I have a Ph.D. in psychology, and I want the opportunity to learn more about Eastern approaches to behavioral change and spirituality."

I won't bore you with the rest of the details, but each step of the way, Doctor threw up another reason why we were being ridiculous. Regardless, I persisted, and he finally agreed we could stay.

He looked me straight in the eyes: "But this month doesn't count," he said.

When I heard those words my insides tied in knots. I knew just how much I had done since our arrival, and I also knew that it was considerably more than anything that anyone else had done. I took a deep breath and looked him in the eyes. "If those are the conditions, I gladly accept."

I then made a request of him. Up until that moment I had been "Bob." I was a nothing-special resident just like everyone else, and I wanted to keep it that way. So I asked Doctor to please continue calling me Bob and not Dr. Sherman. In India they fall all over themselves with salutations and titles.

Doctor heard me and, of course, never called me Bob again. He told me to come to his office the following morning after I completed my morning practices. For the next seven and a half months, Doctor did an excellent job of pushing all of my buttons. I felt like I was in a residential treatment center in which I was in therapy twenty-four hours a day without any break. I was physically ill for the entire stay. During that time, a dog had bitten me, and I had to undergo surgery when my leg blew up from the infection. I also had to have rabies shots in a hospital so unsanitary that I was sure it was going to be the end of me. I had all of this, but fortunately, along the way Doctor threw in a whole lot more at no extra charge.

GOLDEN TEMPLE - AMRITSAR, INDIA, 9/75

CHAPTER SIXTEEN
Yoga

In 1975, hot yoga studios weren't on every corner in America, and accurate information about the various practices was hard to come by. Yoga does indeed come in many flavors, and the variations are described in the ancient text, the *Bhagavad Gita* (one translation of the title is "The Song of the Lord"). Some forms of yoga have a religious underpinning, and some do not. Regardless, all forms assert that there exists a non-material component to our being that is called *perusha*, the Sanskrit word for spirit. The religious forms all believe that this spirit is a part of God. The non-religious forms leave God out of the equation.

All forms of yoga agree that our experience does not affect the spirit within us, and that the spirit is immortal. All of our spirits remain in factory-new condition forever. All forms of yoga also agree that the spirit is the source of our ability to be conscious of our experience. A metaphor that is often used is that of a projector and screen in a movie theater. Everything in the theater is matter. The film can run through the projector, but it is only when the bulb in the projector is on that the audience can become aware of the contents of the movie. Think of the bulb as the aspect of our spirit that allows us to become consciously aware of our experience. The "bulb" in this metaphor (our individual spirit) is the only thing in the room that is not matter. The fact that the contents of the movie do not affect the screen illustrates how one's experience does not affect his spirit.

All forms of yoga seek to provide the practitioner with a path to achieve enlightenment. Enlightenment is defined as the liberation of the individual spirit from being intertwined with matter. Yoga suggests that each of us is really the spirit within; however our egos create *avidya,* a form of ignorance about this. The forms of yoga that have a religious underpinning suggest that after enlightenment the individual spirit merges back with God. Non-religious yoga practitioners believe in two possible outcomes: One is that our individual spirit merges with all the other liberated spirits, and the other is that our individual spirit, once liberated, just hangs out as consciousness. All forms of yoga include the ideas of reincarnation and karma.

The Yoga Institute teaches Classical Yoga. Around 2500 BC, a man named Patanjali wrote about Classical Yoga in *The Yoga Sutras.* Classical Yoga is a form without a religious underpinning, and is composed of eight steps. Steps one through five are Hatha Yoga. Steps six through eight are Raja Yoga. Hatha Yoga is primarily concerned with preparing the body and mind to be able to do Raja Yoga. One of the difficulties with the way that many places teach yoga in the West is that they tend to teach just the physical practices without the philosophy or the other four components. The technology of Hatha Yoga has the potential to provide the practitioner with a state of health that is not considered possible in the West.

Western medicine has a concept of resistance and immunity, but we are only just beginning to explore and understand the factors that would cause one person to become ill and another to remain healthy when both have been exposed to the same pathogen. Our concept of psychosomatic illness is undergoing modification as it becomes clearer that the interaction between the mind and body is far more complicated than originally thought. Yoga asserts that it is possible to attain a state in which one does not get ill.

I'd bore you to tears if I went into full detail about each of the steps, so I'm going to provide a brief outline. Please keep in mind that steps one through five are all geared toward preparing the body so that it does not get in the way of steps six through eight. Steps six through eight are concerned with working on the mind so that it can learn how to concentrate, meditate, and finally reach enlightenment.

> Step One — *Yama*: restraints: There are five components concerned with thoughts, speech and behavior.

Ahimsa: non-violence in thought speech and behavior

Satya: speaking only the truth

Asteya: non-stealing

Brahmacharya: sexual restraint

Aparigraha: non-covetousness

Step Two — *Niyama*: These are observances or practices.

Sauca: absolute purity

Santosa: contentment

Tapa: fortitude

Svadhyaya: self-study/introspection

Isvarapranidhana: resignation to the will of the absolute

Step Three — *Asana*: the physical postures. Vegetarian diet and hygiene practices.

Step Four — *Pranayama*: control of bio-energy primarily through breathing practices.

Step Five — *Pratyahara*: restraint and control of the senses. (Just to give you an example, one learns how to not see with one's eyes open or to not hear.)

Step Six — *Dharana*: concentration. One begins to train the mind to focus on only one thing and stay there.

Step Seven — *Dhyana*: meditation. Just to point out the arrogance and ignorance in the West, step seven is where the practice of meditation *begins*. That means one has already mastered non-violence of any kind, can turn his or her senses off and on at will, and can focus on one thing.

Step Eight — *Samadhi*: the ultimate in
consciousness of the absolute. At this point
one can master all aspects of material reality.

On a typical day at The Institute I practiced the
asanas from 6:15 to 7:30 a.m. I'd then do some
chores for Doctor, meet with him from 8:30 to 9:15
and have breakfast. I spent every morning in silence
except for when I was with Doctor. In the next hour
I took a class, and following that I worked on one of
my special projects. At noon, I ate, and if I could, I
indulged in a brief nap. In the afternoon, I again
worked on a project. I worked on my own practice
in the early evening, took a class before dinner and
then headed to bed. I followed this schedule every
day except on Sundays. On Sundays I did my
morning practices and then participated in the
Sunday morning talk that was open to the general
public.

Living at The Institute had many profound
effects on me. For example, before we began our
adventure at the Yoga Institute, my relationship with
what I believed to be my sexual needs at age twenty-
eight was that—one way or another—I "needed" to
have at least one orgasm every two weeks. Within
that period of time, if I had no sexual activity I
would have a wet dream. I thought nothing about
this when we first started living there. After about
three months, it dawned on me that I hadn't had an
orgasm for the entire time. What was even stranger
was that I didn't even think about it. And, no, there
was nothing special in the food.

On our first day in the twenty-one day better living course, our instructor had recorded some measurements of our bodies, including a gauge of our grip strength. Three months later, I became the instructor for the class, and after taking the same measurements for my students, I decide to re-test my grip strength. In the interim, I had done only yoga and no other exercise. I had lost approximately twenty pounds, so my expectation was that my strength would have gone down. I found it fascinating that my strength had increased by more than thirty pounds.

The processes in yoga help one gain much greater control of one's nervous system. This increased control can manifest itself as a wonderful state of calm and provide significantly improved concentration. Practitioners may also have the ability to alter bodily functions such as blood pressure and heart rate.

The notion that my experience has not altered my spirit has had a profound effect on my self-perception. I have been emphasizing the tremendous negative impact that shame can have. My shame had me believing both consciously and unconsciously that I was inherently flawed. The notion that I am not the Bob Sherman that my ego would like me to believe was quite radical. The possibility that in reality I am a pristine spirit is antithetical to any component of shame. As this notion became more of my reality, I was able to significantly alter my self concept. In addition, this became the foundation from which I related to all of my clients. The unstated reality for all of my clients is that they have a therapist who is always talking to the part of them that is whole and undamaged.

CHAPTER SEVENTEEN
My Gifts From Doctor

When Doctor first told me to come to his office every day at 8:30, I had no idea that this was anything special. I only found out a couple of weeks later when one of the other residents took me aside.

"Does Doctor really talk to you?" he asked.

"Yes. Why?"

"He doesn't talk to *anybody.*"

My conversations with Doctor were usually about specific aspects of Yoga or Eastern approaches to therapy and change. He rarely talked about himself or his own personal capacities. Every so often, though, I did get a glimpse. Monday nights he taught an asana class just for men. During one such class he demonstrated a posture that to this day I still believe is physiologically impossible, even though I saw him do it. In my subsequent research I have never been able to find a photograph of this posture. The closest that I have ever seen is for a posture named *gorakshasana,* but this one is much easier because the feet are facing forward. Doctor sat on the floor and put his feet together so that the bottoms were touching each other. While keeping his feet together, he turned them so that his toes were now facing towards his body while his feet were still touching. Doctor then sat on his feet so that they were directly under his buttocks and also flat on the floor. His legs were bent at the knees and they rested flat on the floor, as well. Please do feel free to try this pose. Just make sure that your health insurance is fully paid and you have the number of a great orthopedic surgeon on speed dial.

My childhood training at the Charlie Sherman Institute of Demoralization rendered me wonderfully capable of finding someone else's defects. For eight and a half months, I tried to find Doctor's. The more time that I spent with him, the more I realized that his reactions and responses to people were never the same. It became clear to me that, from the very moment of the very first day we'd entered the grounds of The Institute, Doctor had played me like a sitar. He had known exactly how to push my buttons, and he gave me the room to see how I would respond. He didn't do this out of animosity. He was only trying to honor my request to find my path to God.

I was lucky that Doctor appreciated my sense of humor. Perhaps this is a sign of his defect, but I prefer to think otherwise. For as long as I can remember, I have used humor as one of my survival techniques, and Doctor liked to laugh.

As I have previously noted, I felt like I was in twenty-four hour therapy. One morning I decided to give myself the treat of sleeping until 7:15. I got up and did all of my chores and then showed up at Doctor's office at 8:30.

"So, you've been doing your practices every day?" he asked.

For the previous four months, my answer would have been yes. But he'd never asked on any of those days, and he had no overt way to have known when I had gotten out of bed.

I'd found a teashop three blocks from The Institute. Every chance I could, I went there and had a couple glasses of chai and some Parle Gluco cookies. These were my caloric sins. On one Sunday afternoon I met another of the students there. He was an Indian advertising executive who was living in Chicago and had come to stay at The Institute for a couple of months. He was upset with The Institute for "forcing him" to do some "garbage exercises" when what he really came there for was to learn how to meditate. I spoke to him and explained why he was being taught what he was and that he might consider learning how to walk before he insisted on breaking the four-minute mile.

After I'd been out, I always stopped by Doctor's office to ask if he needed anything, so that's what I did upon returning from the teashop. He told me that everything was fine but he then said, "The talk that you just had with Shivde (the executive's name) did him a lot of good."

"How do you know?" I blurted. There was no way for him to have knowledge that I had talked to anyone. No one else from The Institute had been at the teashop, and I'd returned to The Institute before

Shivde had. Doctor, being true to form, acted like I had never spoken.

I know that the greatest gift Doctor ever gave me was sharing his time and self with me. He was a concrete, living example of a wonderfully evolved being whom I could believe. But since I'm still a work in progress and a greedy materialist, I will characterize my next experience as his best gift to me. About six months into our stay, we were at the Thursday evening class on the philosophy of yoga that Doctor taught. As usual, all of the students sat on the floor facing Doctor. I sat down and began to take notes. As I was doing this, I began to have a strange experience. A wave of energy began flowing over me. I noticed it and kept on participating in the class. But the wave grew stronger, and it finally reached an intensity that I could not ignore. I soon found myself unable to write. I put down my notebook and closed my eyes. For the next forty minutes I was immersed in what I can only describe as a sea of love. I was vaguely aware of the class going on as normal, and I was sort of aware when the class ended. I didn't leave the room. After a few minutes, I was able to get up and go outside. I felt the effects for the rest of the evening. The next morning, I was determined to find out what had just happened.

"Doctor, please break the rules this time and tell me what happened last night."

"Yes, I did notice that you looked a bit unusual."

"Please, not this time. Just this once. Please tell me what happened."

"What was your experience?"

"At first I started to feel a warm and lovely energy that I have never felt before. As the class progressed, the energy kept getting stronger. It got so strong that I had to stop writing. I felt like I was immersed in a sea of love that was all encompassing. It stayed with me even after the class ended."

"Just look at it as a natural outgrowth of our relationship."

Doctor would not say anything more about what had taken place.

As far as I know, no one else in the room experienced that vast sea of love. I've had similar moments since then, without Doctor present, that I do not attribute to him. Each of these occasions has allowed me to enter a state of being that transcends simple faith, experiences of direct contact with a process that may or may not be divine. Either way, that process is certainly greater than myself, and these experiences fit nicely into my spiritual belief system.

Regardless of the accuracy of my interpretations, I know that I would not have been able to endure subsequent challenges without my spiritual foundation. This truth only reinforces for me the reality that, even if my interpretations are only figments of my deluded ego, they sure do work.

In 2006 in Denver, Colorado, I had another experience that came close to replicating the one I've just described with Doctor. My current wife, Beth, has done a lot of work with a wonderful organization named PeaceJam. That organization holds weekend gatherings for three hundred students and one Nobel Peace Prize winner. In 2006, PeaceJam celebrated its ten-year anniversary and held a gathering for three thousand students and ten Nobels. PeaceJam asked me to be one of the photographers for the event.

The Dalai Lama was in attendance at this event, and during one of His Holiness' talks, I was positioned at the corner of the stage about twenty-five feet to his right. As I started to take pictures, I became aware of a lovely energy emanating from him as he spoke. The Dalai Lama kept talking, and I paused to absorb the exquisite wave—just as I'd done back at The Institute. This time I wasn't surprised by what was going on. I just wanted to absorb as much as I could. I took the photo, "Lama's Glow," on page 155 a short time after that wave had ended.

***

Doctor and I had one point of contention. The yogic approach is one that seeks to control the expression of emotion. Practitioners believe that the more one expresses emotion, *the stronger* the tendency will be to express that emotion. I have always strongly disagreed—at least as it applies to the Western mind and culture.

As a Western therapist, I deal with the negative effects of suppressed emotions both in my clients and in myself. I have seen the significant benefits of tapping into emotions and allowing them to flow.

The metaphor that I use with my clients is that emotion is an energy that dissipates as a result of being expressed. It's like a large boulder being tossed into a calm lake. The initial effect is quite pronounced, but as the ripples go farther out, they decrease in size and amplitude until the lake is once again calm. If the ripples are not allowed to move, they will be stored as potential energy and they will indeed move just as strongly once the restriction is removed.

I believe that the key is to get in touch with both the emotion and its source and allow the emotion to flow. Once this happens and the source is removed, there is no inherent reason for that emotion to repeat itself or increase in intensity without cause. Once a person has reclaimed the energy that had been used to hold things in check, he or she then has that energy to use in more self-enhancing ways. I don't believe that any emotion is inherently bad. The behavior that it evokes can certainly be appropriate or inappropriate.

As long as I'm on a psychological roll here, I'll go a bit further. I also believe that in order to truly give something up one must first have it. Most of my clients have some degree of shame exerting a profound influence over their relationships with themselves and others. Please remember that shame is the belief that there exists some inherent defect in a person's being that makes him feel less than fully loveable. Shame can cause a person to believe that he must hide his "defective" characteristics from others in his life. Essentially, he believes he must deceive others in order to get the love and acceptance that he wants and needs.

I will address the significance of shame and how that relates to my understanding of the spiritual quest in subsequent chapters. I believe that when one attempts to circumvent certain psychological and emotional components of his experience of who he is, these components will ultimately continue to rear their ugly heads until they are resolved. Keep in mind that the emotional components are a function of the individual's false sense of his identity and his or her experience of being hurt or damaged. The act of suppressing these emotions is a "spiritual bypass"—that's what I call it anyway—and, more often than not, such bypasses don't work. Perhaps a good example of this is when a person claims to forgive someone for an offense but deep inside he or she continues to feel angry.

Here's another way of conceptualizing the dynamics that I'm trying to describe. Many of my clients have issues with their own anger. They can be full of rage and express it in inappropriate ways. Or they can be terrified of expressing it for fear of turning into "The Incredible Hulk." My belief is that anger is not inherently bad. I describe it to my clients as the emotional equivalent of pain. Pain certainly does not feel good, but it serves the vital function of alerting us to some physical problem. Once the source is healed, the pain goes away. If humans did not feel pain, our society could not function; the only way we would know if someone were ill would be when he or she died. We would not be able to drive our cars. We wouldn't even be able to go grocery shopping, because corpses would block the aisles. In a similar way, anger serves to alert us to some situation that is not to our liking. The purpose of anger is that it signals us, and it gives us the energy and motivation to take an action. Once the action has remedied the situation, the anger disappears.

My usually unstated agenda for my clients is to assist them to no longer feel "damaged by the offense." If a person can feel truly whole, there is no reason at all to feel anger. As any basketball player can tell you, "No harm, no foul." When we can get to a place of healing our past wounds, we will no longer feel damaged. From that place, we will certainly have nothing to feel angry about and can more easily attain contentment. We can also advance spiritually because we will no longer feel the weight of our shame. In my office, there is a cartoon with a quote from a Tom Robbins novel, *Still Life with Woodpecker*. It says, "It's never too late to have a happy childhood."

***

When I was working with Doctor, I had a strong desire to learn how to give up my ego. Doctor explained to me that ego is an inherent component of the mind. This means that as long as I have a mind I will also have an ego. Essentially, I would need to learn how to use my ego to destroy my mind. These are my words and not Doctor's.

We left The Institute in June 1976. By the time we left, I had lost a lot of weight but had gained some strength. I knew I felt far mellower than I had when we first arrived. I had become a vegetarian and remained so for the next twenty-four years. I knew I had a very different perspective on life and had received far more than I had expected.

We returned to the U.S. in August 1976. On our return, we stopped to visit some friends who were living in Los Angeles. Our first night there they suggested that we go out for a new ice cream craze called Baskin Robbins. As I sat in the passenger seat, I became aware of feeling anxious about the speed that my friend was driving, so I asked him if he would please slow down a bit. My friends remembered me as someone who views speed limit signs as suggested minimums. After my friend stopped laughing, he told me that we were only going thirty-five miles per hour. At that moment, I realized that I had changed in more ways than I was consciously aware.

***

What did I know? I knew that I had just spent two and a half years out of the country and that it was now time to get a job. I knew that I still was not very happy in my marriage, and that I had to work harder at being what Natasha needed me to be. While we were at the Yoga Institute we had very different experiences, and we did not spend a lot of time together. Sex was off the menu at The Institute, so that was not a potential source of conflict. As we traveled after we'd left The Institute, I certainly didn't feel the same degree of anger and unhappiness, but I still did not feel the loving intimacy that I craved. I knew that if we were going to have children, we would need to start fairly soon and that it was my job to make the conditions right. I knew that I wanted to get closer to my mother and help her experience a richer life. I knew that my father didn't like me, and I was starting to become more aware that I didn't like him either.

LAMA'S GLOW
DENVER, COLORADO, 9/06

CHAPTER EIGHTEEN
India: My Spiritual Home

I have no idea what transformed within me that allowed me to have such a remarkably different experience in India when I returned in 1975. The one thing that I was aware of from the start was that India was the first environment in which I experienced people living their faith. My experience in New York was that religion was something that "happened" on certain days or in specified places. Once people left that realm, they went back to their "normal" lives. In India, I witnessed people living their faith and beliefs consistently.

Within the people of India, I observed a sense of contentment. By the time I had left the States in 1974, I had already spent a lot of time in the poorer sections of New York City. In the sixties, I did some volunteer work in Harlem at Northside Center for Child Development with Kenneth and Mamie Phipps Clark. I worked in the South Bronx. I was familiar with what it felt like to walk the streets there. I knew the angry and dangerous vibes that permeated the fabric of those environments. But in

India, even though I often walked in vastly impoverished areas, I did not feel anger or danger. And I was flagrantly using camera equipment worth more money than many of the people around me could imagine. I would walk through the poorest of slums, and people would freely talk, smile, and joke with me. Children played with the most rudimentary toys, and they appeared to be having fun. Both men and women worked very hard, but rarely did I hear anyone complain. I felt a strong desire to better understand their contentment.

Over the years, Varanasi has become the place where I feel the closest to God. Indians refer to Varanasi as "the Chicago" of India, but I have been there at least nine times, and I have never been in any danger. Over the centuries, Varanasi has also been named Kashi and Benares, depending on who was in control. The saddest thing that I have seen over the years has been the dramatic increase in pollution of the Ganges there.[1] I would say that up until the year 2000, I would go in the river. Today I would strongly advise against it. But the river remains quite clean (and very cold) at its source in the Himalayas near Gangotri. It is also fine in Rishikesh and Haridwar.

The real action in Varanasi takes place at sunrise. Two activities are my favorites: One is to wake up around 4 a.m. (okay that's painful) and have a cup of tea at the same teashop I have been visiting since

---

[1] To watch an interview with me about the Ganges on Indian TV, visit www.wanderinghinjew.com/photos.

1974. At that time of the day, only an occasional bell of a rickshaw punctuates the silence. The kerosene lamps give off a wonderful glow. The chai tastes great. On a side note, in 1989 I arrived in Varanasi in late January at night. I had not been there since 1983. The next morning when I walked into the teashop, the owner looked up, saw me, and handed me my tea the way I like it without my saying a word. I laughed and said to him, "You know, we are growing old together," and we both laughed.

Every morning just around sunrise a tour bus (usually filled with Japanese tourists, though, as of late, there has been an increase in Koreans) arrives and stops in front of this teashop. As the tourists climb out of the bus, locals swarm them. The boatmen question, "Boat? You want boat?" Others ask, "Massage? You want massage?" As they do this, they hold out their arms in what looks like a gesture to shake hands. However, once they have you in their grip, they attempt to rearrange the bone structure of your hand by holding on tight and never letting go. Others are selling the most ridiculous of items. There is an epic tale in Indian culture named the *Mahabharata*. It starts with two great armies facing each other for battle at sunrise. Outside the teashop there's a "mini-bharata" that goes on every morning, and I can't tell you how funny it is to watch those unsuspecting tourists attempt to extricate themselves from the swarm.

My other favorite activity is to walk along the Ganges and chant. In 2007, I was in Varanasi with my younger son, Noah, and we came upon a group of men singing some chants before sunrise. Their lack of passion struck me, so I walked over and appointed myself the leader of the choir. Within minutes we were doing Shiva justice![2]

Indian culture frowns upon any public display of affection. I'm sure that this is in the process of changing, but when I took my girlfriend to India in 1999, I warned her in advance that we wouldn't even be holding hands in public. Nevertheless, deep affection does occur in its own forms. For example, the image on page 161 is entitled "The Girls." I took it in Varanasi in March 2003. In it we see people praying, eating, washing and more. We get a glimpse of their community that meets every morning. Now imagine that this scene goes on for more than an hour across a couple of miles.

Hindu's want to be cremated in Varanasi so that they can have their ashes thrown in the Ganges. They believe that this ritual can result in the liberation from the need for rebirth. I took the picture on page 162, "Ganges Glow," in Varanasi during March 2003. In the lower left corner, smoke rises from a *burning ghat*, one of two sets of stairs along the river at which cremations are performed. This one is the smaller of the two. The burning ghats are among the few places in India where picture taking is not allowed.

In 1989, I had an experience at the larger ghat that had a profound effect on me. One day I

---

[2] Noah videotaped part of this scene. You can view it at www.wanderinghinjew.com/photos.

witnessed a woman's passing. That same woman was carried to the river where she was bathed and then wrapped. I believe some spices or incense were also placed on her body. She was then taken to a pile of wood at the ghat, and the wood was set on fire. Her body looked like a hot dog on a barbecue grill. As the flames heated her body, her thighs began to swell. The gases or juices inside her legs caused them to pop open. I am providing you this graphic detail not to be gruesome. This scene was not gruesome at all. As I watched it unfold, it became clear to me that what I was watching was a piece of meat roasting on a grill. Whatever had been the source of that meat's ability to think, feel, and be aware was clearly no longer present. I do not know how to put into words how I knew this or how clear it was to me as I watched.

THE GIRLS
VARANASI, INDIA, 2/97

GANGES GLOW - VARANASI, INDIA, 3/03

Every morning there is a gorgeous sunrise along the Ganges. You can see an example of this in the image "Puja Sunrise" on page 167. In that shot, we see a teen-age boy performing his morning prayer ritual. If you are facing the river, the sun rises directly in front of you. The "Praying Man" on page 168 is my favorite image from India because it symbolizes my spiritual experiences there. I took it in February 1997. You will see in subsequent images from Varanasi that there are steps that lead to the water. What is amazing is the number of steps. I am not exaggerating when I tell you that the water level can vary by over forty feet throughout the year. I was standing at sunrise on one of the wide landings that form part of the flight of steps (I took the shot of the dwarf on page 112 on a similar landing.) As I gazed at the sunrise, I noticed the man in the photograph walking towards me. I took a couple of pictures of him as he approached because he was staggeringly thin, yet striking. We gazed at each other and non-verbally said our *Namastes.* Namaste is Sanskrit and means, "That part of God that resides in me honors that part of God that resides in you." Typically one bows when saying this *pranam* and has one's hands together with fingers facing upwards. We smiled a knowing smile at each other. We were two old friends greeting each other, yet we had never met. When he reached me, he took off his shirt and started to honor the rising sun. He was very much aware that I was taking this photograph, and he did not mind at all. In the shot you will see what looks like a string hanging along his side. That *Yajñopavītam* has many different possible meanings. It used to be reserved only for the Brahmin caste, the priests. Now it can have many other meanings, but they all involve leading a life of purity in thought, speech, and action. At that time, I did not have a digital camera, so I could not see the image on an LCD screen immediately after I had taken it. Nevertheless, I knew that I had captured the moment that I wanted. When he was done, I thanked him for allowing me to share the moment with him.

During March 2003, I took the image on page 169. This time I was in a boat on the Ganges. I was about fifteen feet from the lady in the picture. You may notice that I have named this photo "Indian Mikveh." A *mikveh* is a Jewish public bath that is used for purification. Part of the Jewish ritual involves the necessity of women going to the bath after childbirth or the conclusion of their menses. I guess that in ancient times this served a necessary purpose. However, I find the use of the *mikveh* prior to going to Synagogue to be a very useful metaphor for my clients. For Orthodox Jews, it is essential for a man to go to a *mikveh* prior to going to Friday night service. He does this in order to restore his soul "to its pristine state" so that it can enter the house of the Lord. Most, if not all, of my clients cannot conceptualize the possibility of such restoration. Once they begin to even consider the possibility that there is a part of themselves that has either been totally unaffected by their experience or can be restored to a "factory-new" state, possibilities seem to open up for them.

The image that accompanies "Indian Mikveh" is "Mikveh Reflection" on page 170. These two photographs are the only ones in my collection that I created to be seen together. While they both are complete in themselves, they evoke a more profound experience once the viewer realizes that the second image is of the lady's reflection in the water directly in front of her. Up until now, I have only liked two of my photographs rendered on canvas. "Reflection" is one; "Youthful Senectitude" is the other.

India is a place in which a lot of crazy things happen. Some of these things defy Western logic. One morning I was on one of many boats floating down the Ganges in Varanasi. I wore traditional Indian clothing and was an insignificant speck drifting down the river. Then all of a sudden I saw a cow walking down a flight of stairs eating a garland of marigolds. A man sitting in front of the cow also caught my attention. I picked up my camera and knew that I was about to take an extraordinary photograph. But here came India. As soon as I picked up my camera, the man in the shot covered his face with his hands. I was about three hundred yards away. The hands in front of the man's face ruined the shot. There was no way or reason that he should have even seen or noticed me, but as soon as I put down my camera, he dropped his hands. We did this dance three times. Unfortunately, as we were dancing the cow continued to walk down the stairs, and my boat continued to drift down the river. This drift dramatically changed the perspective of the shot. As my boat reached the point where the moment was going to be totally lost, I made one last attempt, and for reasons unknown to me, the man did not raise his hands. The photograph I did get, "Garland Cow," is on page 171.

About an hour later, I was walking along the river looking for this man. As I approached him, he started talking to me before I could say a word. "It really is rude to take someone's picture without first asking," he said.

I looked at him. "You are quite correct. I apologize for my rudeness."

Once again, here came India. The man and I spent the next day discussing the essential aspect of loneliness on the spiritual quest. The photograph on page 172, "Reverie," is of this man. Ron Fricke directed a documentary named *Baraka*, and this man is in it. If you ever see the film, he is the yogi who is pictured walking out of the Ganges.

Anyone who has ever spent time in India will have a multitude of stories like this. I don't pretend to understand why these things seem to happen with increased frequency there. I just know that they are an integral part of the true experience of India. In the *Star Trek* TV series they had a *holodeck* where one could go and program any experience in 3D. I refer to India as a spiritual holodeck.

PUJA SUNRISE - VARANASI, INDIA, 3/03

PRAYING MAN
VARANASI, INDIA, 2/97

INDIAN MIKVEH
VARANASI, INDIA, 3/03

MIKVEH REFLECTION
VARANASI, INDIA, 3/03

GARLAND COW
VARANASI, INDIA, 1/97

REVERIE
VARANASI, INDIA, 1/97

CHAPTER NINETEEN
"Real" Life Begins Anew

When we returned to the States in 1977, jobs as a
psychologist were a bit difficult to find.
Nevertheless, in a relatively short period of time I
found a position as a psychologist in an experimental
program that was a joint venture between the New
York State Department of Mental Health and the
State Division for Youth. This treatment program
was housed in the Bronx Psychiatric Center. The
intent of the program, which was restricted to Class
A male adolescent felons, was to offer these young
men an opportunity to undergo therapy while they
were in jail. One of my duties was to travel all over
New York State to interview prospective residents
for the program. One of these interviews was with a
fifteen-year-old member of the "Five Percenters."
The Five Percenters started as an offshoot of the
Nation of Islam. This particular young man spewed
a lot of hatred toward white people.

After listening to about twenty minutes of his
venom, I showed him the ring that the Sufi in Iran

had given to me. "Have you ever seen anything like this before," I asked him, pointing to the inscription.

"Yeah, it looks like Arab writing," he said. "I can't read it."

"It says, 'Property of Allah,'" I told him.

In psychology, cognitive dissonance is the mental stress an individual experiences when he or she holds two contradictory beliefs. I asked the kid what he thought about a white guy wearing a ring that said, "Property of Allah." He got stuck in a loop in which he looked at the ring and then at me. I thought of the *Star Trek* episode in which Spock asked an "evil" computer a question that could not be answered. As the computer struggled with the conundrum, it began to overheat and eventually caught fire and "died." Well, this kid didn't catch on fire, but after about two minutes, he finally said, "I got it….You ain't white!"

My experience at the jail provided me knowledge of an astounding variety of heinous crimes that no one should ever hear about. Individually the residents were quite likable in the controlled environment of the jail, but I would never want to meet any of them on the street. As their therapist, I had no difficulty finding a place in them that was just as human as anyone else. The reality of the situation, however, was that what we did therapeutically didn't matter; as long as they were going back to the environments in which they were raised, they really didn't have much of a chance.

I was able to "get out of jail" after three and a half years, when I took the position of Chief

Psychologist at a large community mental health center in Lakewood, New Jersey. I found the job listed in the *New York Times*. I was on probation for ninety days when I began, and therefore I had to do the "Dr. Sherman" thing really well and very straight. I have been quite fortunate in that I have the ability to speak fluent "doctor," so it wasn't much of a strain. The ninety days went by without any negative incidents, and after that I was safe. That position of safety allowed for the following incident to take place.

Every so often one of our staff psychiatrists would conduct an in-service training. One of these was about the latest treatments for schizophrenia. After he gave his talk, I engaged the group in a discussion. I was curious why so much of the content of schizophrenics' hallucinations often involves religious themes. I casually mentioned that in Farsi the word for a holy man, *masteed*, is the same as the word that is used to describe a drunk. I recounted a story told by Ram Dass in which he had given a holy man ten times the normal dose of LSD, and the man didn't appear to be fazed at all. I spoke about the reality of different levels of consciousness, and I speculated that, perhaps because our culture does not have a framework for mystical experience, it might be the case that some schizophrenics are caught in a different level of consciousness, and they have no way of getting back to our "zip code." The group seemed fascinated by what I was talking about. What I later learned from the director of the center was that immediately after the meeting had ended, the psychiatrist stormed into the director's office and demanded that I be fired. The director told him that, since I was off probation and had been doing a great job, that wasn't going to happen.

There was one other time when I mistakenly started to talk about different levels of consciousness that almost got me into deep trouble. In order for me to be able to keep my job as the Chief Psychologist, I had to procure a license to practice in New Jersey. That involved taking a written and then an oral examination. The written exam was not a problem. When I was scheduled for my oral exam, there was a lot riding on my success because if I didn't pass, I would be out of a job. So I knew that I had to be a really good "Dr. Sherman" during the exam. Two people interviewed me at Rutgers University. The first ten minutes went well, and then I really put my foot in my mouth. One of the interviewers asked me how I would handle a certain presenting symptom, and I said, "It would depend on the level of conscious awareness of the client." As soon as the words came out of my mouth, I knew that I was in very deep doo-doo. One of the guys jumped on me like brown on rice. In 1980, psychologists did not use terms like level of conscious awareness. He wanted to know what I meant and what other levels of conscious awareness I knew about. I must have looked like my life was coming to an end as I tried to back my way out of the situation. Both interviewers recognized my discomfort, and the one who had been asking the questions told me that he was in the process of trying to start a division for transpersonal psychology in the American Psychological Association, and I should feel free to talk freely because I was "among friends." I spent the rest of my "exam" talking about my synthesis of yoga and Eastern spirituality with Western psychology. I had dodged another potentially lethal bullet.

I remained the Chief Psychologist for about three years. The position offered me a wonderful opportunity to grow as a therapist and also as an administrator. But for most of that time I was reluctant to enter into private practice. Even though I was supervising many therapists and had a big case load myself, my perspective was that I didn't think that I was good enough as a therapist to be in private practice. Why? I wasn't certain that if I was a patient that I would want to see someone like me as a therapist.

All therapists have an opportunity to treat a wide range of clients and presenting problems, but each therapist is better at helping with some types of problems than others. I believe that it is important for a therapist to know his or her limitations. I have always had my own internal guidelines about what those limitations are. I use the same standards today as to whom I will and won't see. For example, I don't see children, and I don't treat eating disorders. This guideline or rule is nothing personal against kids or people struggling with eating disorders; I just don't feel as qualified at this time to treat children's issues or the complexities that go along with eating disorders.

After about three years, I finally felt like I'd passed my own internal test. Maybe I was good enough to open my own office. My timing was interesting. I resigned two weeks before my first mortgage payment on our first house was due, and we had a three year old and a newborn. But the universe was with us. Within a month, I had a full practice and a waiting list.

***

May You Always Be Filled With The Energy Of Love And Live In The Presence Of Peace, Fun, And God.

If Not, Try Dancing, Rollerblading, Bungee Jumping And Cheese Danish.

(My holiday card 1997)

CHAPTER TWENTY
Kids

In 1978 we had just returned from a three-week trip in which we had gone back to the Yoga Institute in India. We had decent jobs, and we weren't getting any younger. We had always known that we wanted to have children, and somehow we'd been wise enough to wait until we deluded ourselves that we were ready. Getting pregnant proved to be surprisingly easy. Staying pregnant was sadly another story. Natasha had a miscarriage. This was a significant loss for us, and it made getting pregnant again a more worrisome experience. It also allowed me a glimpse into my mother's devastating pregnancy history. Fortunately, our second pregnancy went very well.

Since we were a new-age couple, natural childbirth was *de rigueur*, and we had to take an eight-week Lamaze course. I have never been in the presence of so many couples who were so attentive to each other. It all looked like heaven. Three years later, we needed a refresher course because we were getting ready to have our second child. This time I found myself in a class with tired looking people who were mostly cordial with each other. I'm sure there is a lesson here someplace.

With our first child, the Lamaze classes taught me how to be a breathing coach, and I felt up to the task. So when I found myself in the labor room, I sat down next to my wife and gently put my arm on her shoulder to get ready to begin a soothing "cleansing breath."

Natasha swatted my hand away. "Don't fucking touch me! Just stand by the door and make sure no one comes in to bother me!"

I am sorry to report that Natasha was in labor for fifty-five hours. I wish that I had been better prepared to know what to do in that situation; neither she nor our son should have been allowed to endure that much distress.

Despite the struggles, the fifty-fifth hour culminated with the arrival of Jonas Sherman, a glorious specimen of a boy. He weighed nine pounds and was twenty-one inches long. At birth, he looked just like my uncle, so I felt fairly confident that he was mine. He was jaundiced and a bit colicky, so he had to undergo phototherapy to remove the bilirubin that was causing the jaundice. After a few extra days in the hospital, we took him home. There was just one thing that we had not expected: Jonas was absent when the angels taught how to sleep through the night. Perhaps his fifty-five-hour attempt to come into the world had prepared him for a fighter's existence. For the first four months, Natasha and I took turns staying up with him. We had a Snugli baby carrier, and I often walked the street at 2 a.m. with Jonas strapped to me.

I won't carry on about Jonas; he's in his thirties now, so that would take a while. I'll just share a few things that come to mind. I did find myself sad that I couldn't breast feed him. I found it such an astoundingly beautiful experience that I wished I could have shared with him. I had to settle for bath time. When he was old enough to not be afraid of the water, he loved his baths. And all the goofy splashing along with the delicious smell of his soapy soft skin was pure heaven for me.

When Jonas was five or six months old, his "home" was a mesh playpen that sat in the middle of our living room. I happened to be home the first time he was able to stand up. He was not aware that I was watching him. He crawled over to one side and jammed his head into the mesh. Because it was soft and pliant, it easily bowed out. He then continued to push his head forward into the soft wall. As he did this, his forward movement redirected his head upwards. No matter how many times he slipped, he remained determined. Eventually, he was able to force his head high enough so that he could reach up with his hands and pull himself to a standing position. Joy emanated from him. The same was true when he started to walk. I had the opportunity to witness the astounding amount of determination he brought to this task, as well. No matter how many times he fell, he picked himself up and kept on doing it until he could actually take some steps.

What is clear to me from these examples is that we're all brain damaged from the number of times that our heads hit the floor. But more importantly, we are born with an amazing determination and desire to blossom and grow. In his innocence, Jonas was not burdened with any thoughts of shame or inadequacy. No one stood there telling him what kind of klutz he was for falling or how many attempts it should have taken him to stand up or walk. And he didn't have an inner voice to tell himself that, either. The distance from that place of innocent determination to where most of us internally live as adults can be devastatingly far. The toxic burdens of our internal critics keep many of us from ever being free to experience our human potential. I know that my own critics profoundly affected me, and so I couldn't help but transfer some of that burden to my sons.

> *For this (and a few other things) I am truly sorry. I know that I am powerless now to do the work for you that will allow you to root out the sources of your own internal voices. I pray that as each of you continues to knock out the dents that I inflicted on you, I am able to participate in any way that I can as a source of validation. I'll even pay for a new paint job.*

One of the best-kept secrets about parenting is that none of us knows what we're doing. We all make it up as we go along, and we often model our improvisation after our own parents. One of the most shocking moments of my life came when I was yelling at Jonas for something, and I heard myself say, "If you don't stop that crying, I'm going to give you something to cry about." This was a line directly from my mother's mouth. When I was a kid, it didn't make sense to me, and I swore that I would never say it to my own kids. As soon as I heard myself say this, I immediately started to laugh. A few moments later, I choked up with tears.

I had been frustrated and angry with Jonas because he cried too much and too loudly. As this annoyance within me grew, I started to become aware of the fact that the problem wasn't Jonas; it was me.

***

Three years and another miscarriage later, Noah joined our family. Prior to his birth, I couldn't imagine that he would look any different than Jonas. It seemed to me that, since the same genetic material was joining together again, it would produce the same result. I was wrong. If Jonas was the fighter, Noah was the lover. One day when he was five, we had the following conversation. "There must be something terribly wrong," he said.

"I'm sorry. What's the matter?"

"I'm not having enough fun today!"

Another time, when he was nine, he said, "What should I be when I grow up? And I don't want to hear any of your psychologist bullshit about whatever makes me happy. This time just tell me!"

"Okay, I want you to become either a neurosurgeon or a stockbroker so that you can make a lot of money so I can retire."

"Thank you."

About five days later we were walking into a local mall.

"I've been thinking about this neurosurgeon and stockbroker stuff," he said.

"Well, what do you think?"

"I think that you ain't getting shit."

***

When Jonas was about eighteen months old, we took him to a park. His eyes lit up when he saw a large playground slide. He ran over to it and started to climb the ladder to the top. As I watched in proud admiration, I became aware of my wife yelling at me.

"Grab him!"

She was concerned that he would fall because he didn't know what he was doing.

I pointed to Jonas, who was about half way up the stairs by then. "He's fine," I said. "See, he knows exactly what to do."

"Get him!"

I climbed up behind him just to make sure. He was down the slide and heading for the ladder again before I'd even had time to climb back to the earth.

Maybe fathers tend to overestimate and mothers tend to underestimate the capacities of their kids. In looking at this from the point of view of a psychologist, I would say that this might be because mothers are always trying to protect their kids, and maybe sometimes they are unconsciously trying to keep their kids dependent. Men, on the other hand, get off on accomplishment. They may have difficulty with what they might experience as weakness, and they don't want to see that in their kids. Of course, this is a generalization and not always the case.

That day was somewhat of an anomaly in that I was able to assert my point of view, and Jonas was able to fully enjoy the slide. I am sorry to say that, as time went by, I was not able to continue that pattern. As the division of labor progressed, my job became to make the money, and Natasha's job was to take care of our kids.

I don't want to give the impression that Natasha was a bad mother. She was devoted to our kids, and she did everything that she could to take care of them. But just as I did with my own issues, she couldn't help but burden the kids with hers. I let our boys down by not taking a firm enough stance against some of the things that I knew were not in their best interests. The reality of the situation was that I had an adversarial relationship with my own wants and needs—the few that I was aware of—and I did an equally poor job of taking care of myself. This does not in any way absolve me of the fact that I let my kids down. The reality that I was doing the best that I could with what I knew doesn't diminish the consequences to my kids.

As time went by, the consequences of our unhappiness as husband and wife built to the point that we began family therapy. We used the excuse that we were having difficulties with Jonas. In truth, Jonas' behavior was a symptom of the shame issues that Natasha and I had brought to our marriage.

CHAPTER TWENTY-ONE
A Brief Visit to Weirdland

When we returned to the States in 1977, we learned that one of our close friends, Ron, had a serious health issue. He was an artist, and he had developed a form of glaucoma that was resistant to treatment. As a result, he was going blind. Since Western medicine was not helping, he resorted to seeing an energy healer named Yolanda. I agreed to go with him to a class she was teaching at the United Nations.

One evening I found myself in a conference room at the UN. Twenty-five people sat at a large table. Yolanda was at the front of the room. At some point, a woman in the room asked Yolanda for some help with a health problem. Yolanda asked her to sit in a chair separate from the group. Up to this point, all was well. But I entered weirdland when Yolanda asked me to sit in a chair facing the lady. I have no idea why she singled me out; I'd had no previous contact with either the lady or Yolanda. Yolanda then asked me to tell the lady what was wrong with her.

I looked in her eyes and smiled. "I'm sorry. If your diagnosis is now in my hands, you should consider buying life insurance." I turned to Yolanda. "I don't have a clue," I said.

"Look at her," Yolanda said. "Hold your hands up with your palms facing her."

I did as instructed, but I still had no idea.

"Tell her what's wrong! Pay attention to the information you are getting from your hands."

At this point, I realized that this Yolanda nut was not going to give up until I gave a diagnosis. So I focused my attention on my hands, and without touching the lady, I moved my hands in front of her and "scanned" her body.

"Your lungs don't feel the same to me," I said.

Yolanda nodded. "Tell her what you mean."

"You have a mass in your right lung."

I have no idea where my "diagnosis" had come from. I said what popped into my mind just to get out of the situation. I am glad to report that this appeared to be good enough for Yolanda, and the rest of the class proceeded without any other incidents. I didn't have any further contact with Yolanda until about six months later. We went to a going away party for Ron. He was a Canadian citizen, and he was moving back to Canada to be closer to his family and to have access to better health coverage. His glaucoma was getting worse, and he would soon be blind.

When we entered Ron's apartment, Yolanda was there. She immediately came over to us and began talking to Natasha. "Don't worry. This one will be fine," she said.

We both looked at her like she was crazy because we had no idea what she was talking about.

She looked at us in astonishment. "You're pregnant with a son, and you will not miscarry."

Natasha and I looked at each other and laughed. All we knew at the time was that we had just started attempting to get pregnant again, and hadn't told anyone that we were even trying. Turns out that when we had bumped into Yolanda, Natasha and I had conceived Jonas just four days prior. Once the pregnancy was confirmed, I decided that I wanted to see Yolanda again.

I saw Yolanda in her apartment about four times. On each occasion, she would put her hands on me and I would feel a lovely warmth, which led to an overall feeling of comfort throughout my body. As she worked on me, Yolanda would tell me that I was a wonderful healer. I would laugh at this, but it was fun to go to her house for these visits. On one occasion, I brought my brother with me. When she put her hands near his head, she told him that he had a "cold spot." This became a running joke between us. When Ritchie was about ten, he fell off of his bike and had a concussion. We joked that his "cold spot" probably resulted from this. While I'll never know what Yolanda was actually referring to, Ritchie died of brain cancer about thirty-two years later.

During one of my visits to Yolanda, she told me to lie down at one p.m. the following day and she would "visit me." The next day, I did as she had asked and had the amazing experience of feeling the exact same warmth that I would feel during our sessions.

***

In August of 1982, I attended an administrative meeting of the upper echelon of the mental health center where I was working. It was a typical, boring Thursday afternoon meeting that usually had no relevance for any of my concerns. What made this meeting unusual was that, for reasons unknown to me, I had what felt like a panic attack. I had never had a panic attack before, and I was unaware why I would be suddenly having one. Fortunately, I had the presence of mind to do what I had been teaching my clients to do. I did some breathing exercises and I used self-hypnosis to re-establish a sense of calm.

I remember that it was a Thursday because I used to work late on Thursdays and would always come home in the afternoon to have dinner with my kids.

During my brief time at home, the phone rang, and it was my father's girlfriend. With some difficulty she informed me that my father had died earlier that afternoon. My father had been in the hospital at that time, but we didn't think he would pass away. In fact, he was scheduled to leave the hospital in a couple of days. It immediately became clear to me that what I had thought was a panic attack was, in fact, me "feeling" my father's death.

At the time, I had no way of understanding what was taking place, but experiences like this have become an integral part of my perspective on the world we live in. I now know that more goes on around me than just our limited understanding and interpretation of the material world.

CHAPTER TWENTY-TWO
Fire Walking, Bungee Jumping, and Sky Diving

The period between 1983 and 1993 was perhaps the most personally challenging and productive for me. I was fortunate in my private practice to have a waiting list of potential clients. Once I had made the internal decision that I was finally "good enough" as a therapist, I was not at all worried about my ability to take care of whatever needed to be done. What I didn't realize was that I wasn't worried at all—about anything.

I had read about a fire-walking workshop that was being held nearby, so I signed up. During that workshop, the instructor asked us to write down a list of our fears. As I sat there staring at a blank sheet, I consciously decided that I needed to lie so that I wouldn't be the only one with an empty paper. I wrote down the no-brainer lines about fearing death or disability. The truth is that I didn't have a clue about what I feared. I was that out of touch.

The fire walk was wonderful. We started the fire and made a bed of coals. The instructor told us that

Toyota engines are made from aluminum heated to 1,200 degrees and that our fire was about 1,400 degrees. After two hours of preparation, we were ready to walk. The instructor cautioned us to walk slowly and not hurry as we traversed the coals so that we wouldn't trip. The process we went through would spare our feet from burning. Tripping and planting one's face in the coals, however, was another story.

As we readied to walk, I told the instructor, "There's no way that I'm not doing this, but there's no way I'm going first." Well I went third, and I was amazed that it didn't even hurt. I have since walked across coals nine times. On one occasion, I got a very small blister, and I have no idea why that happened. In subsequent workshops, I think that I got more pleasure out of watching the other members of the group go through the process. I enjoyed watching the transformation from fear to elation on their faces. I'm sorry that I never thought to take pictures of those glorious moments. I'm also pleased to note that I no longer have to lie about my fears, but to list them would require a whole, separate book.

In the mid eighties, I completed my first skydive. After a day-long course, five of us and an instructor got into a very small Cessna that had no rear seat. We all sat on the floor of the plane and waited for it to reach five thousand feet. The instructor informed me that we would be jumping based on weight. I was the heaviest, so I would jump first. I then learned that I would not be jumping directly out of the plane. Instead I was to step onto an eight-inch metal plate, grab the strut under the wing and pull myself out. Yes, ladies and gentlemen, while doing this I was essentially flying outside of the plane. I can't tell you how much fun that was. I actually motioned to the instructor to let everyone else jump first because I wanted to spend more time flying on the wing. He didn't have a good sense of humor about this, and so when he said to push off, I did.

I believe that the biggest surprise for me was that, when I approached the door of the plane and looked outside, I did not experience any fear. Instead, I only noticed how far away the ground looked. From that perspective, I really had nothing to fear, because I would only get hurt if I hit something. I do have a fear of heights, but I was so far away from the ground that my mind understood the experience as stepping out into nothingness.

About five years later, I did another jump. This one was from 13,500 feet, and another diver videotaped me as we fell. From this height, I experienced two minutes of free fall before I had to open the chute. On the video, I have a smile on my face all the way down. I experienced an unparalleled sense of joy and freedom.

Bungee jumping presented another opportunity to experience a similar kind of freedom. But I must admit that I felt more nervous doing this than I did skydiving. Obviously, with bungee jumping the jumper is closer to the ground, and if the cord breaks, he or she can do nothing about it. The most interesting jump I've ever done was from a cage suspended from a crane at about two hundred feet. Bungee jumping provides a double thrill. You get the experience of the swan dive, but then, when the cord is stretched to its limit, the force hurls you back into the sky.

All of these activities are not necessarily sane. When I was doing them, I was aware that I was seeking a rush. I now believe that I was also unconsciously preparing myself for the work I needed to do on myself. I would strongly recommend fire walking because, of the three, it is the safest. It is also a marvelous opportunity to confront one's fears and to experience a greater capacity for connection to the divine than we normally believe we have.

CHAPTER TWENTY-THREE
Bad Therapists — Good Results

As the 1980s progressed, the tension in our household increased. We had two wonderfully intelligent, creative, and very active sons. Their existence allowed Natasha and me a wonderful opportunity to get in touch with many of our own unresolved issues. We also did not necessarily see eye to eye on how to deal with certain issues. This prompted us to enter into family therapy. Within a relatively short period of time, however, family therapy turned into marriage counseling.

I'm not sure about the competency of our family therapist. I am quite certain, however, that as a marriage counselor, he made one judgment that had devastating consequences for me. During the time of our therapy with him, Natasha told him a secret. No, it was not about having an affair. His error in judgment was that he did not insist that she tell me this secret. Instead, we carried on with our therapy. I did not learn the contents of this secret until two years and two therapists later. This third therapist had the good judgment to insist that Natasha tell me the secret. I would like to suggest to any therapists reading this section that, if you have a client who shares a secret with you of such devastating significance, you insist that your client share the secret with his or her spouse, or you no longer participate in the therapy. (I realize that I have not told you the contents of "the secret." This is a book about my life. The secret is Natasha's and not mine to share.) Our first therapist's failure to do this made our therapeutic process a sham because Natasha and I had no way to resolve our differences until I knew the secret that was having such a profound influence on our relationship.

As my title for this chapter implies, however, I did receive a special gift from this first therapist. During one session, our therapist made the offhand remark, "There's no doubt that your father was an alcoholic."

"There's no doubt that he wasn't," I said. "What would the significance be if he had been?"

The therapist suggested a number of books that I could read that would allow me to get an answer to my question. This prompted me to explore the emerging literature on adult children of alcoholics. The possibility that my father might have been an alcoholic had never occurred to me. I don't remember ever seeing him drunk. I do remember a few occasions when he had passed out on his favorite chair after combining some prescription medications with alcohol.

The therapist's suggestion that my father had a problem came long after his death, so I decided to contact one of my uncles. I was blown away when my uncle started the conversation by saying, "There's no doubt that Charlie was an alcoholic." I hadn't even brought up the subject yet.

"Where the hell were you thirty years ago when I needed you?" I asked.

"Drunk," he said.

As I learned more about the effects of growing up in an alcoholic environment, I began to identify myself as a child of an alcoholic. I began attending ACOA (Adult Children of Alcoholics) groups, and I also entered into individual therapy with a woman who was supposed to be a specialist in this area.

At my first session, she came into the waiting room and said, "Come on in Jim, Bill or whatever your name is."

I felt put off that she hadn't even taken the time to check out my name, but I didn't confront her about this. I had a habit of not acting in harmony with my visceral responses, and I would need to address that issue in therapy, but not with this specific therapist. She was far too impressed with herself and far too invested in the fact that she knew she was going to be moving out of the area. She did not initially feel the need to share this information with me. However, during one of our sessions, she also provided me with a gift. I was regaling her with recent events at home. I was certain that my explanations of what was occurring in my marriage were justifying my anger at Natasha.

"What did you want from her?" the therapist asked.

"How about a morsel of compassion or caring?" I said. "If I were lying stabbed and bleeding on the floor, I feel like she would just step over me and continue walking."

"Did you ask Natasha for what you needed or wanted from her?"

A stream of profanity raced through my head. I couldn't believe that my therapist would make such a ridiculous suggestion. But she was indeed correct. I did need to learn how to ask for what I wanted and needed. My ability to do this would take a few more years because I first had to get in touch with my wants and needs and then I had to deal with my adversarial relationship with these wants and needs.

"You are living in a world in which you are pursuing being right," the therapist said.

Again, she was correct. Part of being "right" meant, to me, that I had to do everything at a certain standard of quality. Another part involved doing things "in the right way." My therapist helped me discover that my pursuit of being right tended to make whomever I interacted with feel wrong.

"Very often in life, you are going to have to choose between being right *or* being happy," she said. "More often than not, you can't have both."

I have come to very much appreciate this last tidbit of wisdom.

***

About five years later, I was in a men's group led by a female therapist. After the group had been well established, she invited a male co-therapist to join the group. During one session, I related details about a strange event that took place between a woman who I had been dating and me. (This particular session took place about three years after I had gotten a divorce). As I spoke, the male co-therapist got up, stood in front of me and started shaking his finger and yelling at me. This was no therapeutic ploy. He was furious, and I was shocked. I did not respond at all to this therapist during the group. At that time in my life I was not yet comfortable with expressing my anger. I needed a few days to marinate in the experience so that I could become aware of the totality of my reactions. At the next session a week later, I told the group leader that I had something to say. I stood up and walked in front of the male co-therapist.

"You were very inappropriate with me last week," I said. "If you ever stick your finger in my face again, I will break it!" The rest of the group was very silent. I then spontaneously turned to the female leader. "And where were you, Mom, when this asshole was doing his thing?" This was a direct reference to the childhood environment that I had grown up in. I had never been able to confront my father in this way, and it was also true that my mother was not capable of stopping my father.

***

Wisdom Lies In Choosing Being Happy Over
Being Right.
Faith Lies In Trusting In The Beneficence Of
The Universe.
Fun Lies Somewhere Between Death By
Chocolate And The Kama Sutra.

(My holiday card 1999)

CHAPTER TWENTY-FOUR
Wonderful Therapy — Lovely Results

From 1987 through 1994 I suspect that I spent enough money in therapy to buy a few cars and perhaps a summer home for a number of therapists. As it became clearer to me that I didn't have a clue about many significant aspects of my being, I became more determined and focused on dealing with whatever personal issues came into my awareness. This pursuit led me to some wonderful and sometimes weird techniques. I did Holotropic Breathwork with Stanislav Grof. I did bioenergetics, traditional therapy, rebirthing, and a few other things along the way. Of all the things I did, the one that had the most profound impact was a series of intense experiential workshops at a wonderful place named Spring Hill. Spring Hill was both the name of an organization and a place in Massachusetts. I had learned of Spring Hill in the waiting room of one of my more far-out therapists when I read an ad for a workshop called "Opening the Heart" in a new-age magazine. The brief description of the workshop intrigued me, so I decided to try it.

My goal for the weekend workshop was to see if I could relearn how to cry. When I saw that the workshop was being held at a Hindu temple, I began to laugh. What a delightful cosmic joke! The workshop started on Friday night, and by Saturday afternoon I found myself sobbing on the floor in front of a statue of Ganesh. By the time the workshop was over, I had received the special gift of getting in touch with my deeply felt childhood sadness, and I was able to cry for that, as well. The weekend was so helpful that I wanted to take every workshop Spring Hill offered.

A couple of months later, I attended another Opening the Heart workshop. This weekend was probably the most transformative weekend of my life. These workshops can be quite intense. Participants have the opportunity to get in touch with whatever unexpressed emotions are tucked away in the recesses of their beings. At that time, my reservoirs held an abundance of anger and sadness. The workshop started on Friday evening and ended on Sunday afternoon. On Sunday, the forty-two participants broke into seven groups of six individuals with one leader. Our leader had us hold hands and visualize a white light above us. I had never had success with these types of visualizations. So, as I rolled my closed eyes, I took a deep breath and sighed knowing this would be a waste of my time. I was shocked when I began to see a white light that was in fact coming down and bathing me. I sat there in amazement, just taking it all in. The leader asked for a volunteer. I was still way too busy inhaling the light. We then widened the circle, and the volunteer lay down on the floor in the middle. The leader sat at her head and asked her to take deep breaths. There were six other people in the room doing similar things in their own groups. At that time in my life I had never experienced anything like this, and I was curious to see what was going to happen. In a relatively short period of time, the woman on the floor was letting out a sound that seemed to come from the accumulation of all the pain in the universe. And there were six other people concurrently letting out their version of this pain. This lasted for about ten minutes, and then we tightened the circle once the volunteer had rejoined us. We were asked to visualize the white light again, and our leader asked for a second volunteer. "I'll do it!" I heard myself say.

As I lay on the floor it occurred to me that the previous woman had looked like a scene from *The Exorcist*. All that was missing was the green slime coming out of her mouth. Something welled up from deep inside. The more I got into the breathing, the less aware I was of what else was going on around me. I was, however, aware that the wailing in the room had resumed. Whatever was inside of me that was being aroused grew in intensity, and I became further lost in the experience. As it traveled up my throat, my last thought was, *here comes the green slime*. I was totally blown away when what came out of me was pure joy. I had never before experienced bliss in such intensity. This bliss lasted even after I'd completed the exercise. I was able to go back to the circle and hold hands. I was able to again experience the beauty of this white light. But my day was not yet complete. As I was sitting there in a state of bliss, I felt a tap on my shoulder. The strange part was that nobody was behind me. So I ignored the experience until I felt another and firmer tap on the same shoulder. I opened my eyes and turned around. No one was there. I closed my eyes and started to chuckle, but then, to my total amazement, I felt a hand resting on my shoulder. I began to sob. I will leave the explanation and interpretation of this experience up to you. I can assure you that no one was there, and I am not in any way exaggerating or distorting what happened. What I can tell you is that after that moment, I no longer felt alone.

***

When the workshop ended, I couldn't wait to get back home in order to share my experience with Natasha and to show her "the new me." At that time, the more work I did on myself, the more I began to realize the deep sense of shame that had been controlling my existence. The man whom my wife had married had existed as if he had committed some unknown sin for which he needed to atone. He had an almost total lack of awareness of his own wants and needs. In many ways he was ashamed of being a man. The man who was driving home after that workshop wanted to be seen. This new man no longer needed to hide who he really was.

Unfortunately, my return home did not go as I had hoped. I so desperately wanted to share what had taken place over the weekend. I wanted to offer Natasha a different kind of love that came from a place of desire rather than an opportunity to "earn" a sense of worth. However my experience of transformation did not result in our ability to share in any deeper mutually satisfying relationship. So for the next year, we continued marriage counseling and I continued my own personal journey.

***

My work at Spring Hill also went through a transformation when the staff invited me to complete some volunteer work in preparation for me to become a part of the staff. I had to take an intense weekend training to become a facilitator for the specialized workshops they did for survivors of sexual abuse. In my private practice, many of my clients were incest survivors, and it had become a subspecialty for me. This weekend training was arduous for the participants. So as the workshop was coming to a close, the staff decided to give us a going-away present: a guided meditation led by one of the female staff members. We all sat or lay on the floor and closed our eyes. In a soft voice, she recalled the intensity of our weekend and reminded us to leave the pain and suffering behind as we embarked upon our journeys home. The more she described the pain we were leaving and the love and joy we were going to, the more my insides started to ache. She instructed us to visualize the warm, loving reception that we would get when we finally returned home. At that moment, my insides twisted into a knot. All I could visualize was more futility. An intense scream welled up inside me. Fortunately, I had the presence of mind to bury my head in a pillow. I then found myself involuntarily screaming at the top of my lungs, "No more!" The meaning of the scream was instantly obvious to me. I had unconsciously made the decision to separate from Natasha. I wish I could say that I had the ability at that time to know where my boundaries and limits were and that I had consciously decided to separate. But this was far from the truth. My reality was that I did not know where that limit was until it overwhelmed me.

I don't believe that I have the capacity to adequately describe the seismic shift that took place inside me as a result of that scream. For a very long time, I had done all that I possibly could to make our marriage work. My reality was that I knew it was my job to do whatever was necessary to "fix" it. As the echo of that scream left my awareness, my reality changed to the fact that, even if it was my job, I was no longer capable of the task. I had simply run out of gas. I saw an attorney the following day. Even at that point, I was not seeking a divorce. My attorney informed me that the state of New Jersey did not recognize legal separation. But we formulated a plan to arrive at a formal financial agreement so that it would be clear what I was going to contribute financially to Natasha and our children. The idea was that, if we ultimately did seek a divorce, this agreement would serve as the foundation for the financial settlement of that divorce.

I mistakenly believed that, because Natasha and I were two reasonable people, we would simply work out a financial agreement. I wanted to move out within three weeks, but that timeframe turned into eleven months because each of us had a vastly different concept as to what constituted a fair agreement. During that period, we went back to our marriage counselor to discuss how and when to tell our kids what was happening. I wanted to tell our kids immediately so that they would have plenty of time to adjust to the situation. I wanted them to know right away that our separation did not mean that they were going to lose either one of us. Our therapist disagreed with me. She believed that we should wait until two weeks before I moved out; anything longer, she said, would be confusing and painful for our kids. They were eight and eleven at the time, and I did not feel as though I had the expertise to be sure about my position. So I agreed to not tell our children until two weeks before we knew I was going to move out. I'm fairly certain that my kids would say that was a mistake.

The day we finally did tell our kids was horrible. We all sat in our living room together, and I told them that their mother and I were separating. Noah looked shocked and overwhelmed. Jonas picked up a log that was laying by a wood-burning stove and began smashing it into the floor. At that moment, I felt both horrified and encouraged. I was certainly pained to see him so distraught, but at the same time, I admired his ability to express his anger. After a short period, Noah told us that he could not tolerate being in the house, and he ran out. In less than a minute, our older son told us that he was going out to find and be with his brother. Again I had the contradictory feeling of deep sadness that my sons were going through this experience and gratitude that they had a way of sharing it that my brother and I never had when we were their age.

***

I wanted our kids to know that I was not disappearing from their lives, so I rented a house close enough for them to walk to. I'm grateful to Natasha that she allowed them to participate in my move. She also agreed to let them stay with me that first weekend.

During the eleven-month period in which we were struggling to arrive at a financial agreement, Natasha informed me that she was aware that this was not going to be merely a separation. She was right. Three months after I moved out, we were divorced. Four months after that, I bought a house on the same street as the one I had been renting. The process of moving in and decorating these two homes proved to be a most rewarding experience for me. For the first time in my life, I was able to create the kind of physical environment in which I wanted to live, and I relished the opportunity to create an environment for my sons that would offer them an opportunity to experience increased freedom in a far more relaxed setting. It is a source of great sadness for me that I was not able to create that environment for them any earlier. As I said in my dedication, because I regard this as an act of unsuccessful parenting, I am always ready to help them pound out any dents they received along the way. In other words, I'll pay for their therapy.

***

The Key Is To Risk Being Seen.
To Live In Harmony With Your Voice
That's Always Been Inside Of You.
That's What Will Allow Your Soul To Fly.

Of Course, A Thoroughly Satisfying Sex Life
And Regular Bowel Movements Don't Hurt Either.

(My holiday card 1996)

CHAPTER TWENTY-FIVE
Marriage: Part Two

Without pain and desperation, ignorance and fear keep us stuck in familiar, comfortable territory. By comfortable I don't mean easy. Most of us experienced some degree of pain in childhood. As a result, we have also learned ways to deal with that pain. These coping mechanisms can be severely put to the test during certain milestones in our lives that offer us disguised opportunities to grow. Some of these include the first time we leave home, the births of our children, and when our children start to assert themselves. This list is far from exhaustive. One of the most potent opportunities is when we get married.

We are not born with instruction manuals. What is really scary is that our parents don't have manuals either. For many different reasons, the environment we live in as children becomes our "normal." It makes no difference if our friends' environments are very different from ours. As a kid, I used to watch "Ozzie and Harriet" and "Father Knows Best." I have no idea why Jim and Ozzie always wore sweaters—as did Mr. Rogers. What I did see were fathers who were home much of the time and who were quite active in their children's lives. My parents never watched me play little league baseball. My father only saw me play basketball one time, and I could never figure out why he came to that game. It never occurred to me to ask why he didn't come to my games on a regular basis. I simply assumed it was not important enough and therefore I was not worthy of his time. Shame is a deeply felt sense or belief—conscious and or unconscious—that one is deeply flawed in one or more ways. Shame arises as a result of negative childhood experiences. Children do not have the capacity to properly understand these experiences, which they can only interpret as their fault. Shame can easily become a part of the "normal" experience of a child whether or not the child is consciously aware of it. Shame is easily created if our parents criticize or comment on our being rather than our behavior. Telling a child, "I don't like that behavior" has a much different effect than saying, "You're a bad boy." Negative comments on one's being create shame. Shame makes us uncomfortable to let others see us—naked or not.

Later in life, shame may prompt us to hide certain aspects of our selves. We may function under a conscious or unconscious belief that others will not love us if we unveil our true selves. In essence, we live knowing that we need to con our way into getting someone else to love us. Incidentally, this is why some people experience their relationship with their dogs as their most loving. For these people, the total absence of shame in their dogs and their dogs' total acceptance of them allows them to feel safe enough to love their dogs without fear.

All of us have an instinctual need to graduate from our parents' institution with a diploma that has two gold seals on it. The seals come from each of our parents, and they signify that we are loveable and worthy. If we graduate with one or both of the seals missing, we *could* spend the rest of our lives consciously or unconsciously believing we are inadequate or defective. Unless we choose to do something about it. Until we do, we will expend a lot of energy trying to fix the defect by earning that missing seal. Without it we believe that we have failed in some way. We will then go through life experiencing negative consequences as a result of our perceived unworthiness and unlovability.

Most of us at a certain point in our lives arrive at a place where we'd like to fall in love and get married. At this point, we all have varying degrees of experience in relationships and some ideas about what characteristics we'd like in a spouse. Some folks believe in the idea of soul mates. This implies that for each person in the world, there is another person in the world who will complete that person and vice versa. When I was a teenager, I remember jewelry stores selling "broken heart" necklaces. There were two heart halves in a pack. The charm on each necklace had a jagged edge, and it fit together with only the matching other half. The sad truth is that two halves don't make a whole in a relationship.

They make two unhappy halves. In my spiritual belief system, we're all soul mates.

Let's say that I'm a guy and I want to marry a woman who is spiritual, intelligent, and altruistic. (Aren't you relieved that I didn't request has great legs and big tits and is also a nymphomaniac?) The qualities I've mentioned are common among many different women, so how or why do I end up choosing a specific woman? How do I know that she is *the one?*

I think people receive a lot more information than they consciously realize. For example, a man enters a crowded party, and he is drawn to a woman on the other side of the room. Perhaps he thinks that he is attracted to her hair. At the same time a woman is attracted to a man's hands or the way he makes her laugh. Sure, there is truth to the conscious reasons why we are attracted to one another, but that's not the whole story. Ultimately, we will pursue someone past the third date and maybe even marry that person, but not just because we are attracted to some quality or feature. Out of a universe of possible choices, we will pick a mate who in time will allow us to recreate a significant aspect of our childhood experience. Interestingly, some people refer to this as chemistry. I am not at all referring to any type of overt behavior. I am referring to the fact that by interacting with our spouses we feel the same visceral sensations we felt when we learned our shame. Those sensations are not the same for everyone. For some it might be a tightness in the throat or a sinking feeling in the stomach. Our intellects will seek to label the experience. For example, we might think that we are anxious, or depressed. The labels may or may not be accurate. It doesn't matter. What is of significance is the sensation, not the label. Often the process of labeling the sensation is part of our attempts at control and actually is a part of what we learned to do to cope or survive the situation.

To give you an example, let's imagine a three-year-old girl who lives with a mother who has a habit of abruptly breaking contact with her child either physically or emotionally. The child might have angered the mother or prompted the mother to feel anxious, so the mother responds by going into her bedroom and locking the door. The child might feel a sense of panic as a result of being cut off. That panic might feel like a difficulty in breathing in her chest or a tightening in her throat. Because the child does not have the capacity to hold the parent responsible for the parent's actions, she experiences herself as having done something terribly wrong. It is also the case that it is a very rare parent who apologizes to the child and makes it clear to the child that "Mommy made a mistake." If this pattern of behavior is a regular part of the child's experience, she will certainly develop a fear of abandonment, and she will also learn that she deserves to be abandoned. Now if we fast forward, and this child is now a married woman, there is a really good chance that her husband will do something that will prompt his wife to feel a tightness in her chest or her throat closing. What he does will probably have nothing at all to do with locking himself in the bedroom. He might, for example, not respond immediately to a text message or he might be engrossed in a football game as she is trying to talk to him. The significant point is that, as a result of the interaction, the woman will feel the same visceral sensation that she felt with her mother, and she will react emotionally as if she is being cut off. The part that I find fascinating is that frequently the husband will be experiencing his wife as inappropriately doing something to him, as well. More often than not, during the course of a marriage, *each* spouse has the repeat of his or her sensation and he or she then seeks to fix it. Most often, the sensation is different for each of the spouses. They may attempt to fix it by changing their own behavior, or they might seek to change the behavior of their spouse. They might have discussions and arguments. Whatever the methods they use to fix things, those methods are guaranteed *not* to work!

By now some of you might be doubting the accuracy of what I'm writing. And some of you might be convinced that I am quite pessimistic about marriage. Please read the rest of the chapter and please remember me when you find yourself ready to kill or be killed. Call me when you are ready to drag your piece-of-shit soul mate into therapy and you hear yourself saying in your mind, *What was I thinking when I married this…?*

Let's now go back to the idea of the missing seal, the notion that it was there to be gotten and that one needs to earn it. The unconscious game plan goes something like this:

If I can put myself in a situation that will allow me to feel the way I felt when I blew it as a child and this time do it right, I will then be a double winner! I will at the same time fix things with my mate and also fix things with the parent who didn't give me the seal. This all sounds possible because after all I'm much older now, and I have learned many things. So I'm now in a position to earn my seals and go on with my new and improved worthy me.

As I have previously written, I don't really have a concept of heaven or hell. The notion of a loving God who would banish his or her children to hell makes no sense to me. However, I do find the metaphor of heaven useful to occasionally illustrate some points to my clients. So with this in mind, I do believe that "marriages are made in heaven." If there is a loving God then He—or She or It—would want his children to grow and realize their full potential. This God would also know that, more often than not, the necessary conditions for this growth are pain and desperation. Frequently, marriage is an optimum pressure cooker to provide such pain and suffering. The "heaven" part is that the marriage provides the opportunity for both spouses to grow.

Sadly it is the wonderful competence of the woman in my example that ensures that she will fail dismally. When we pick our mates we pick *perfectly!* However, it is precisely this perfection that guarantees our *failure.* We do pick someone who will allow us to re-experience those visceral sensations and bring us to our knees. But here's where the girl's flawed logic reveals itself. Perhaps, just perhaps, the reason that the girl didn't get the seal wasn't because she was a fuck up. Perhaps, just perhaps, the girl didn't get the seal because the parent wasn't capable of giving it! Since we pick *perfectly*, we will pick a mate who is equally incapable of giving us the seal! Now you must really think that I believe it's all hopeless. And what in the world does this have to do with heaven?

Remember when I said that people change only in the presence of an overwhelming amount of pain and desperation? That's precisely the point that most people are at when they drag their hopeless spouse into my office to be fixed. I view my job at that moment as to first honor the veracity of some of their complaints. Most of the time it is true that each is doing things that are not conducive to a great relationship. But that's not what Heaven's version of Match.com had in mind when it put these two people together. The second component of my job, for those clients who are open to it, is to help them understand exactly why they put *themselves* in the position they're in.

When I ask a client whether his or her spouse acted this way before they were married, the offended spouse usually gives the answer, "Yes but…" I ask clients to identify the visceral sensations that occur in their bodies in the presence of this behavior and ask them if they had ever felt them before? Some can even trace the sensations to their childhood. When people sense that their marriage is in the toilet—and they can hear the faint sound of a beginning flush—the pain and desperation they experience creates a ripe opportunity for growth.

For those of you who are attached to the belief that the only happy ending to the movie is for the couple to stay together, I would offer the following scenario. In the ideal situation, the husband and wife (or husband and husband or wife and wife) enter into individual therapy (with different therapists) and work on their individual issues. Unfortunately it is not always the case that both are ready to do this at the same time. I would then advise the one who is ready to do his or her individual work. In the ideal situation, after each has done his or her individual work, they then re-enter couple's counseling together and "fire" the other person from the position that he or she had originally hired him or her to do. You see, at this point neither person will need an external source for the seal. If each person's individual treatment was successful, each person will have learned how to give himself or herself the seal. The couple would then be ready to enter into a new contract for a different relationship with each other.

If only one member is ready or willing to do the work, a husband for example, he absolutely should do it. After he has gotten his seal, he will have some choices to make. Is he willing to accept the maintenance of the same relationship? If so, he will be doing that from a place of choice and not deficiency. If not, is he willing to give his spouse more time to get to a place of being able to work on her own issues? If so, the "one who waits" needs to take full ownership of the consequences of that choice and not blame the other for not yet doing the work. The other choice is to end the marriage. For me, that last choice is not one to be taken lightly, but it is also not a sign of failure. The marriage was entirely successful in offering the opportunity for growth. Neither spouse is responsible for what the other does with that opportunity. It may also be the case that the spouse who was not ready may need more time (translation: more pain and desperation) in order to get to that place. That opportunity might only be available to that person after a divorce.

I do realize that I have written about marriage and divorce without mentioning the frequent reality of the children involved. Of course, parents should always consider the children's best interests. I don't have a one-size-fits-all blueprint for the children's concerns. My parents stayed together until my mom died. I have no idea how a divorce would have impacted me. My guess is that I would have had an opportunity much earlier in life to begin to understand what was wrong with my "normal." I also know that my relationship with each of my sons improved after my own divorce. If there is a divorce, it is essential for the parents to learn that even if they couldn't make it as spouses, they still have to do all that they can to be effective parents together. The children should never be an opportunity to act out any hurt or anger against the ex-spouse.

After my divorce, I moved into a house that my kids could walk to. Initially Natasha and I did go through the joint custody drill with Natasha being the primary custodian. But eventually my sons opted to move in with me. I had begun to create a very different environment in my new home that was far more relaxed, a lot more fun, more conducive to growth and a positive self image than the one that had existed in our family home. The divorce certainly had some negative consequences for my sons. I would like to think that the positives have outweighed the negatives, but that's not my call to make. It remains vitally important to me to participate in whatever ways I can to help my sons get in touch with those effects and to be available in the process of removing those effects from their lives.

***

Opportunity for growth often
comes cloaked in tragedy and pain.
Our task is to grieve and then seek
out the potential lesson to learn.
So often we are the co-creator of our
experience and not merely the victim.

On the other hand,
if 2012 is really Sarah's year
then Darwin was wrong and
the Mayans just might be right.

(My holiday card 2010)

Our beloved doesn't make us love,
they are the catalyst who allows us
to feel safe enough to show
who we really are.
Sadly they also often become
the mirror reflecting
who we wish we weren't.

(My holiday card 1998)

CHAPTER TWENTY-SIX
Sex: Part II

During April of 1991, Natasha and I finalized our divorce, and I was once again a single man in the world. Dating at forty-five is a fascinating experience. I had never been great at dating, so I did not have a wealth of positive experiences to fall back on.

When I was in high school, I'd always hated making that first phone call. I felt a tremendous amount of awkwardness because of my belief that the success of the phone call was about whether I could "make it happen." This time around, I tried a different approach. I no longer placed the full responsibility to "make it happen" on me alone. When I called a woman whom I did not know well, I quickly filled her in on my apprehension about first phone calls. I asked for help. This simple request often turned an awkward situation into a much easier collaborative effort.

After going on a few dates with different women, I felt myself drawn to a specific individual, and I wanted to see her again. We enjoyed some lovely dates together, and I found myself wanting to leave the sexual desert that I had been inhabiting for a while. I was mildly nervous but mostly excited to be there and very much looking forward to what was about to unfold.

We were sitting on a bench that overlooked the Atlantic Ocean on the Jersey Shore. We started to kiss. Things were progressing quite nicely when I hit an unexpected speed bump.

"I imagine that you're at a point in your life where you want to make up for lost time," the woman said. "You probably aren't really interested in getting seriously involved with someone right now, are you?"

I wasn't in the mood to talk at that moment, obviously, but I also recognized that this woman had presented me with an opportunity to risk revealing myself. I owed it to the two of us to speak my truth.

"That's absolutely true," I said. "I know that I still have a lot of work to do on myself, and I need to do that first before I will be capable of making a serious commitment to anyone."

"Shit!" she said. "I was afraid that you were going to say that. I was so looking forward to taking you back to my place and banging your brains out. Now I don't know."

This prompted me to sit up in a rather different and much less comfortable position on the bench.

Much to my shock she said, "I didn't say anything about asking you to stop."

At that moment I knew that I was no longer in Kansas. I was now having an interaction with a woman who was not afraid to speak her truth, and she was in the presence of a man who was not ashamed of who he was and what he was doing. My expectation of being punished for saying or doing my truth did not come to pass. It was a bit confusing that she wanted to pick up right where we'd left off, but it was so very refreshing and liberating to be with a woman who was taking responsibility for herself and who had the capacity to do so.

However, once again the universe threw me a curveball. A short time later, we found ourselves in bed and very undressed. There I was, naked and lying next to a gorgeous, desirable woman. The magic of making love was about to happen, and I was ready. Then her fingertips made contact with my skin, and my body reacted, not by joining in the fire of passion, but by shutting down. I may as well have been encased in plastic. I wasn't capable of having sex, much less of making love. Once again I found myself drowning in inadequacy and confusion. After a few more attempts that culminated with the same result, I went back into therapy.

After sharing my experience with my therapist, she asked me whether I had ever considered the possibility that I had been sexually abused.

What a preposterous idea.

I knew that I had an affinity and talent for treating people who had been sexually abused, but I had neither considered nor did I have any recollection of having been sexually abused myself.

By this time in my life I was consciously aware of how much of a hypocrite my father had been. He'd always talked about how intercourse was the ultimate expression of love between a man and a woman, but at the same time he'd had multiple affairs. However, I hadn't experienced that hypocrisy as any form of sexual abuse. On the other hand, I didn't have any better explanation for what I was experiencing, so I agreed to attend the next Spring Hill sexual abuse workshop as a participant. I will spare you the details of what took place during that weekend. Suffice it to say that when I returned to my next session after the workshop, I informed my therapist that, while I still had no overt memories of having been sexually abused, I had done an expert imitation of someone who had been. I had experienced a wide range of intense emotions that could not have come from just a place of empathy or compassion for others. I had discovered a hidden reservoir of extraordinary pain and fear.

There were times during the Spring Hill weekend that I was feeling nauseated or anxious. These feelings were not coming from a place of compassion for those around me. At one moment a scream burst from deep within my being, a projectile vomiting of pain and fear that had been buried in some secret place, perhaps a direct expression of what I had felt when I was being abused. A new set of tumblers fell into place, and I experienced a hint of clarity about why I was ashamed of being a man and why I felt a need to atone for an unknown sin. I had unconsciously transformed my experience of being the victim to one of being the perpetrator in an attempt to gain some measure of control in my life. The shame involved in believing that I was the perpetrator instead of the victim was far easier to tolerate or accept than the reality that, as a child, I was utterly vulnerable and dependent, and in that place I had been abused by someone who was supposed to have been my protector. I had unconsciously given myself a reason to feel guilty about having been abused. The underlying unconscious dynamic behind this guilt is as follows: *If I feel guilty, that means that I did something wrong. If I did something wrong, that means that I got what I deserved.* That line of reasoning allows one to maintain the illusion that his or her parent was good and protective. It also allows one to maintain the illusion of control. The thought process is as follows: *If I did something wrong that caused me to be abused, that means that I could have avoided being abused if only I had done the right thing.*

And so I began another intense three-year period in which I did everything I possibly could to confront my shame, my fears, and the various behavioral consequences that resulted from that abuse.

***

Along the way, I was truly blessed to share my journey with some incredibly wonderful women. These women accompanied me through my second adolescence and into my subsequent adulthood. I also met some truly courageous people. Entering into the emotional territory where one can heal from sexual abuse is extraordinarily difficult. I have a great deal of compassion and understanding for sexual abuse survivors who do not do the work. Of course, it is a tragedy that they will spend their lives living the consequences of that abuse, but I can understand how for many of them it is too terrifying to take the risk.

The greatest hurdle most sexual abuse survivors have to overcome is changing their perceptions of themselves. Often they view themselves as irreparably damaged. I don't know how I could have done the work I did on myself without the foundation of my spiritual beliefs. So many times I experienced myself as emotionally falling into a bottomless pit with nothing to hold onto except my sense of faith. Nevertheless, because of that faith, I knew I would get through the process. Now, with my Hinjew belief system, I realize I am a spiritual being who is having a human experience. My identity as Bob Sherman is a construct of my ego's imagination and ignorance. My true identity is that spirit within me that is untouched and unaffected by my experience. My spirit is in the same "factory new," pristine condition that it has always been and always will be.

There is no sexual organ that can dent, scratch, or shatter my spirit.

Perhaps the second biggest hurdle I had to overcome was whether I was ever going to be able to reclaim my innocence. I got lucky in this pursuit when I stumbled onto the realization that I was confusing innocence with ignorance. Consider a child who has just learned how to make mud pies.

He might wake his mother up too early the following morning because all he wants to do is get back to his pile of dirt and water; he knows exactly what he wants. What makes his behavior so wonderfully innocent at that moment is the total lack of shame about what he wants and the total absence of any negative judgment about what that means about him for wanting it. Once I realized that my work required coming to terms with whether my feelings and desires were defective, my task became far less impossible.

The following is a poem that I wrote after I realized I was, in fact, a sexual abuse survivor and when I was in the trenches of recovery. I probably wrote this around the beginning of 1992.

Ode to My Perps

For so long I crawled under the burden of the
heaviness of your existence.
Unable to fly? Afraid to fly? Not knowing it was
okay to fly!
How savagely you attacked and preyed upon my
innocence.
So lost in my love of you and not of myself.

So convinced of my unworthiness.
So oblivious to myself and the inequity of it all.
So sure that you knew better.
So convinced it was up to me.

After all, didn't love and loyalty mean not to notice?
After all, wasn't I responsible to clean up your mess?
After all, doesn't love mean saying yes?
After all, after all.

Awakening to worth made it all start to crumble.
Awakening to truth, what an unbelievable shock!
Awakening to wants and needs.
Awakening to your chorus of no's.

Feeling your increased attempts at suppression.
Feeling your fear of the truth.
Feeling your self-righteous wrath.
Feeling the agony of being next to you.

The fear of stating my truth.

The fear of peeling the façade.
The fear of making a mistake.
Feeling the agony of being next to you.

Out of the desperation emerged the necessity of
change.
Out of the rubble emerged possibility.
Out of the heaviness, the terrible, oppressive
heaviness.
Feeling the agony of being next to you.

On to the unknown world of yes.
How confusing the ease of availability.
How confusing to be praised for things once
condemned.
How glorious to give up the begging.

Now the shock and pain of work yet to be done.
The damage not yet repaired.
Perps not yet in my past.
The unknown horrors await.

CHAPTER TWENTY-SEVEN
Vibes I've Known and Loved

Sometime during 1982 I became interested in the vibrations of things. I had repeatedly heard from my new-age friends that crystals had vibrations that could be felt. I had a piece of rose quartz in my office, and whenever I held it, it felt like a cold rock to me. I would occasionally hold it while I spoke to my clients. One day during a session, I began to feel a strange vibration or energy emanating from my hand and running up my arm. The energy went away when I put down the piece of quartz. There was a flea market across the street from my office with a shop that sold crystals. After work I went to the flea market and was shocked to realize that, when I held different crystals, I could actually discern different vibrations. I had no idea what had changed within me or that I was about to enter a world of energies I hadn't known existed.

One of the therapeutic techniques that I used to help myself deal with my recovery from sexual abuse is something called rebirthing. Rebirthing uses rapid breathing to access alternate states of awareness.

These sessions were intense. I probably got as much of a workout from these sessions as I did from the high-impact aerobics classes I was taking. After these sessions, I began to experience a lovely and unexpected phenomenon. If I held my hands away from the sides of my head, I could feel a strange vibration or energy. This vibration would change depending upon the distance I held my hands from my head, and the experience increased with subsequent rebirthing sessions. After each session, I would lie on a massage table for many minutes playing with this energy field. I found it wonderfully pleasurable.

Eventually I tried holding my hands on the sides of someone else's head just to see what would happen. I was pleasantly surprised when this person reported feeling a lovely sense of well-being. I did not understand what was happening, but I wanted to see if other people would have the same experience. The universal experience was that if I held my hands on someone's shoulders, he or she would very soon experience the same sense of well-being or contentment. Some people even began to experience a decrease in their pain or discomfort. I was, of course, quite intrigued by what was going on. I knew that the therapist that I had been seeing did something called Reiki, and so I asked him if what I was experiencing was anything like what he did. He suggested that I take Reiki training in order to find out for myself.

My yoga practice also produced an energy thread within me. Ever since my training in Bombay, yoga had become a significant part of my life, but because my training at The Yoga Institute was so comprehensive, I'd never felt the need to explore or experience how yoga was being taught in the States. Around 1991, I came across a conference in Pennsylvania in which a number of prominent teachers of yoga were going to give presentations. I must admit it was fun for me to see the interaction of the yogis' egos and what they were teaching. This by no means is meant to imply that the conference was a waste of time. I just don't think we can ever escape some effects of our egos.

One of the yogis was a Sikh who practiced and taught a form of Kundalini yoga. Kundalini is said to be an energy that lies dormant in the base of our spines. Kundalini teachers use a metaphor to describe the effects of the practice: When aroused, a coiled serpent travels up the spine and pierces energy centers known as chakras. The body has seven chakras. My training in yoga had not involved an active pursuit of the awakening of this Kundalini energy, so I was very much looking forward to this yogi's presentation. During his class, he instructed us to engage in some intense breathing. Once again I found myself in the middle of another unexpected gift. His technique worked perfectly, and for the first time, I experienced a profound surge of energy that shot up my spine and "exploded" inside my head. After the conference had ended, I couldn't wait to get back home to see if I could reproduce the results on my own. Much to my surprise, I could.

The energy experiences of Kundalini and Reiki intersected during the course of the Reiki training. During that training, I went through something called an "attunement." I had my eyes closed, and the trainer put his hands on my head. The next thing I knew, a surge of energy shot through my body like an internal lightning bolt. I passed out. Fortunately I had been sitting in a chair, so I'd merely slumped over. At the end of the training, I learned that none of the other trainees had fainted. I was still going to rebirthing therapy sessions with the Reiki instructor, so the next time I saw him I asked him what had happened.

"I don't know," he said. "I was hoping you could tell me."

I found out that when I performed Reiki treatments on others, they experienced many positive things. I also learned that the energy I had been feeling after my rebirthing sessions was similar to the Reiki energy, but it was not the same thing. In addition, I was continuing the Kundalini practices, and that experience was significantly different from either of the other two energy experiences.

My rebirthing therapist and I decided to do an experiment to see if I could replicate my experience of the internal lightning bolt on him. So during our next session, as I was lying on his massage table and he was sitting on a chair near my head, I put my hands on his head and did my thing. He briefly passed out. When we were done, he wasn't sure it really had happened. Luckily, we'd videotaped the whole thing. For the next twelve years, I had a lot of fun sharing my version of the Reiki experience with family and friends. Most people continued to experience a deep sense of contentment and well-being. One of my favorite things was to immediately intervene with someone if they had just burnt themselves. Believe it or not, I found that if I shared the energy with them, they would initially experience an increase in pain, but if they allowed me to continue, most of them would not blister. Other people experienced significant release of emotion. My girlfriend tried to convince me that I could make a fortune because another thing that the energy was really good for was relieving menstrual cramps. She believed that if the word ever got out I'd become an instant millionaire.

I stopped doing the energy work on a regular basis after I realized that whatever I was adding to the Reiki energy was depleting my own energy. I never learned how to keep myself out of the process.

Around 1995, my girlfriend and I went to Atlantic City to go to a casino. I have never spent a lot of time in casinos because I suck at gambling, so it was my practice to decide in advance how much money I was going to donate to the casino's coffers, and then I would just treat the loss as the cost of entertainment for the night. What I didn't expect on our trip to Atlantic City was that, as soon as we entered the casino, I became so nauseated that we had to leave. The moment we left the casino, my nausea went away. I experienced the same feeling upon entering two other casinos, so I knew something was happening that I didn't yet understand. When I shared this experience with my rebirthing therapist, he informed me that he has the same experience. He told me that I was feeling the "vibe of desperation," that sense of despair experienced by the many people who weren't going to be able to make their mortgage payments.

My experiences with Kundalini and other energies reinforced my spiritual beliefs. It is clear to me that there is far more going on in the world than merely what we can objectively measure.

The energy that is available with Reiki can only be used to do good. This energy does not emanate from within the practitioner. The practitioner only serves as a conduit to help another utilize energy outside his or her awareness but that surrounds him or her all the time. Think of it like the tuner inside a radio. We are surrounded by countless radio waves. The tuner does not create the waves; it only allows us to become aware of the contents of those waves.

It is not necessary for a practitioner of Reiki to be physically present with the recipient. If you remember, I shared an experience that took place with Yolanda in which she sent me a treatment. It is through the intention of the mind that a practitioner can send energy to the recipient. This is a clear indication of the power of our thoughts. Try to remember this the next time you are thinking of someone and they call or e-mail you. The Buddhists have a practice that they call *metta*. *Metta* is the practice of sending someone loving kindness. Many religious traditions talk about the power of prayer. Many people have experienced the effects of the laying on of hands. All of these phenomena clearly indicate the interconnectedness of us all. The limitations our sensory organs, ignorance, ego, and fear impose upon us blind us to this interconnectedness and create the illusion of separateness.

I took the picture on page 239, "Before Time," in Malibu, California, during January 2003, back in the days of film and slide photography. I took the shot with Fuji Velvia slide film. At that time, Velvia was a favorite of mine because it tended to overly saturate colors. Different films and manufacturers render images differently, so it was important to be able to match the film to the desired result. With the advent of digital photography, one now has the ability to make these adjustments for individual shots either before taking the shot or while processing the shot. Once again, the dark blue is the real color of the water, and the milky quality resulted from the time exposure.

BEFORE TIME - MALIBU, CALIFORNIA, 1/03

CERULEAN WONDER - PAHUATANI, NEW ZEALAND, 4/10

During April 2010, I had the good fortune to spend two weeks in New Zealand. New Zealand is a country made up of two islands. I believe the total population of these two islands is a little more than four million. The number of sheep may actually exceed the number of people. New Zealand is exquisitely gorgeous. The lakes are pristine.

I took "Cerulean Wonder" (page 240) on the west coast of the South Island. I am rarely attracted to taking shots of the ocean without incorporating something of interest in the foreground. The day that I took this photo was overcast, and generally on such days my camera rarely comes out of my bag. However, I was somewhat desperate because I was not going to be back in this neighborhood any time in the near future. Again, the texture of the water resulted from a time exposure.

On the same day and in the same place, I took the image "Smashing," on page 242. I love this shot. If you compare this photo with the previous one, you can see the dramatic influence of the change in lighting. I took these two shots within a half hour of each other. The first image has lovely shades of blue. But the second image explodes with color. The beauty of the color in the water echoes what's going on in the sky. A small bird sitting on top of the rock appears oblivious to the tremendous force of the smashing wave. It remains so calm in the midst of such fury.

SMASHING - PAHUATANI, NEW ZEALAND, 4/10

CHAPTER TWENTY-EIGHT
Sex: Part III

Under normal circumstances I would not be writing the following. However, since I have emphasized the degree to which my life has been negatively influenced as a result of my childhood sexual abuse, I would like to share the following for those readers who themselves have also experienced some form of sexual abuse.

In 1994, the universe threw me another curveball. At that time I viewed myself as still very much a work in progress in my sexual recovery. I did feel as though I was past "my adolescence" and into my adulthood. Once again, I was blessed with the opportunity to enter into an extraordinary relationship. This woman encouraged me to risk being a full participant rather than just somewhat of a spectator during sex. She assured me that I did not have to worry about hurting her or being hurt. She offered me the opportunity to experience sexuality in a new way.

I could never have predicted what was to follow. During the course of our lovemaking, I spontaneously had an arousal of the Kundalini energy I have previously described. This arousal is something that is sought through the practice of Tantric yoga. I had never studied Tantra, but my awareness of it allowed me to at least understand what was happening even if I did not fully understand why it was happening. At that moment I felt at one with the divine. Sex, which had been for most of my life an intolerable source of pain and shame, had now become a source of beauty and bliss. How do I put into words the light years that separate the horror of sexual abuse from the ecstasy of communion? I had gone from feeling defective to feeling immersed in grace.

I have never shared specifics about my sexual abuse or my recovery with my clients. I have shared with some of my clients the fact that I am a survivor of sexual abuse, but only when I considered my revelation to be helpful to their processes. I also let my clients know that I believe that when a person has experienced horror in a certain type of experience, that person is in a unique position to deeply appreciate the exquisiteness of that same experience under the right circumstances. A person who has almost starved to death may bring a unique sense of delight to a great meal. And someone who has survived a catastrophic illness might learn to live each moment with a sense of gratitude and awe.

In sharing that I am a sexual abuse survivor, I do not mean to imply that I am anywhere near being finished with working on my issues. We are all works in progress regardless of our underlying issues. It is abundantly clear to me that, not only will I not finish my work in this lifetime, I will need perhaps many more lifetimes to reach a place of enlightenment.

CHAPTER TWENTY-NINE
An Interesting Lesson

During the nineties, I took a number of interpretive dance workshops with a woman named Gabrielle Roth. I very much appreciated her teaching style, and I was able to experience my body in a free and fun way. Most of these workshops were held at Omega, a wonderful retreat center located in Rhinebeck, New York.

After registering for one particular workshop, I received a packet that included instructions to bring clothing of the opposite sex to the workshop. It appeared that Gabrielle was planning a dance in which all the participants would cross-dress. I thought this idea to be ridiculous, and so I went to the workshop with just my normal clothing. On the morning of the second day, I started to feel like I had made a mistake in not bringing a dress.

I had nothing to wear to the dance, and I didn't want to feel left out.

About thirty participants were in my specific workshop and another two hundred were taking various other workshops with other instructors at the same time. I went into the dining room at lunch and addressed the crowd.

"Excuse me everybody," I said. "I've got a serious problem that I'm hoping one of you can help me with."

It took a few moments for everybody to stop talking.

"I've got a dance to go to tonight," I continued. "And I need a dress."

Everybody in my workshop knew what I was talking about, but the others didn't have a clue.

"Now, I don't want just any dress. I want something that will work well with my height. And I think I'm a size twelve."

"Who are you kidding?" said one smiling woman from my workshop. "You're at least a size fourteen."

"I'm not sure that's true," I retorted. "I think I'm a twelve with any decent designer."

Thankfully, another woman came to my rescue. She took me to her room and gave me a dress and the appropriate jewelry. Unfortunately, she did not have shoes in my size. I went back to my room and got dressed. I then decided that as long as I was doing this, I was going to get the full experience. So when it came time for dinner, I went to the cafeteria in my dress even though I knew the rest of the people in the workshop were going to change into their cross-dressing outfits after dinner.

When I walked into the dining room, a bunch of women surrounded me. They giggled, fixed my hair, adjusted the dress and taught me how to walk like a proper lady. I enjoyed the instruction and spent my meal eating up the attention. Prior to my grand entrance that evening I had entered that very same dining room at least twenty other times in my life. Never before had a woman bee-lined in my direction. I suggested to my newfound posse that I needed to go home and buy a new wardrobe.

After dinner, I walked to the large room where our dance was going to take place. I was early, so I didn't expect anyone else to be there. However, standing in that room was a tall, thin, elegantly dressed bitch who wore fishnet stockings and high-heeled shoes. I use the word "bitch," because I instantly hated his guts and knew that the room was not big enough for the two of us!

I have never before entered a place and felt the slightest need to check out the other men in the room or what they were wearing. I had only ever concerned myself with whether there were any women in the room whom I might be interested in. I was unconcerned about any other men in the room that might be competition. Dressed as a woman, however, I found it fascinating and shocking that I'd noticed the competition for the first time and felt that I was outmatched.

As a man I know that there are many things that I take for granted that wouldn't be the same if I were a woman. I can remember driving to a woman's place to pick her up on our first date. We had met at a party and did not have a lot of time to talk. After that we only spoke briefly to set up more time to meet and talk. As I was driving to get her, it occurred to me that this woman had no way of knowing whether I was a rapist. My next thought was that it had never occurred to me to be concerned about whether *she* was a rapist.

CHAPTER THIRTY
Being a Therapist

I have been truly blessed in that I really love being a therapist. I anticipate with great joy each opportunity to create a safe environment in which a client may embrace the opportunity to take extraordinary risks. My clients frequently ask me, "How do you listen to this shit all day long?" I usually say, "What makes you think I'm listening? Listening costs extra." But the real answer to this question is that I don't view it as my job to make someone change. Being a therapist is not like being an orthopedic surgeon. If a patient breaks an arm, his or her job is to transport that arm to the physician's office. The physician does all the work of setting the arm and putting it in a cast. All the patient has to do is carry that cast around for six weeks and then the surgeon removes it. I'm not aware of any therapeutic equivalent to this. I view my participation in the growth process as that of a consultant. My clients request my assistance in helping them to gain a more comprehensive and compassionate experience of their existence. My task is to participate in the creation of a relationship based on a deeply felt sense of trust and safety. My task is to let my clients know that they have been heard and understood, and perhaps to offer them the opportunity to reevaluate their experiences from a more adult and informed perspective. But I realize I really have no control over what my clients do with whatever I offer them. If I believed that I should have control, I probably would not have lasted very long as a therapist. I tell my clients: "I am not driving your car, and so I have no control over what you do with what I offer."

Most of the time, I am at my best as a human being when I am involved in this therapeutic process. It is rare for me to get angry or disappointed with any of my clients. My awareness of just how out of touch I have been in my own life makes it easy for me to never be frustrated when my clients "don't get it." I am keenly aware that overwhelming amounts of pain and desperation are required for most people to be able to overcome the inertia that results from their fear. So when I am in the presence of someone who is clearly hurting, a part of me absolutely sympathizes with his or her pain. But another part of me is also aware of the opportunity the distress presents.

I also have to admit that every so often I do hear something that saddens me deeply. I will never cease to be amazed at our creative capacity to inflict devastating pain on one another. However, the structure of the therapeutic environment allows me to feel safer than when I am out in the "real world." Whatever remaining issues or fears I have about the invasion of my own boundaries in the real world do not exist in my office. This safety allows me to be more fully present and to give more to the process without the fear of being hurt.

What my clients are not aware of in the beginning of their therapy is that I am always talking to that part of them that I know is just fine. I have little difficulty in letting my clients know when their behavior is inappropriate or self-destructive. At the same time, I am directly or indirectly differentiating that behavior from their being. My perspective is that who they really are is that pristine spirit that is totally untouched by their experience.

The sun is a sphere that emits light in all directions. There is no dark side to the sun. I suggest to my clients that we have a sphere of love in the center of our chests. At birth we emanate that love in all directions. But then we begin to experience the hurt from the spears that we encounter in life. The pain of these spears causes us to unconsciously erect shields. To varying degrees, these shields do an effective job of protecting us from further pain. But an unintended consequence of these shields is that they block the light within. We can put up so many shields that others can no longer see our light, and we also lose sight of it as well. But these shields do not extinguish our internal sun. If we can become aware of the shields and then risk slowly dismantling them, we can once again reveal our loving nature.

I began seeing a client in the early eighties. She was in her early sixties when I met her, and I still remember our first session quite clearly. She came into my office and introduced herself by telling me her name.

"In 1942, I was diagnosed paranoid schizophrenic," she said. "I agree with this diagnosis but not with the paranoid component."

This woman was intelligent, articulate and creative. Unfortunately she had also been tormented for more than forty years because she believed she was defective. After a number of sessions, I learned that she went to church every day to pray. Her religious beliefs were an integral part of her life.

"Do you believe you have a soul," I asked.

"Of course," she said.

"Do you believe that your soul is ultimately who you are?"

"Yes. Absolutely."

"Do you believe you have a schizophrenic soul?"

Once she realized that of course she didn't have a schizophrenic soul, she began to sob. This was an exquisitely beautiful moment in which she was able to experience her essence as complete and undamaged.

As a therapist, I wait for such moments in which my clients understand themselves in new ways. These moments can also be when I see or feel an emotional opening through which my clients can either get to know a new aspect of their being or gain a different perspective on who they really are. I view my awareness and receptivity to these moments as part of "my artistry" as a therapist. What I now realize is that this is also precisely what I pursue in my photography.

Most of the time when I take a portrait shot, my subject is very much aware of my presence. When I can, I attempt some form of conversation or interaction. What I now realize is that I am engaging in an attempt at connection. I am seeking permission to enter into this person's world, and I am hoping that his or her response will reveal some of his or her world to me. I also am just beginning to realize that, out of all the possible moments that I could take shots, the ones I have been choosing are exactly the same as the ones I look for in my office. Perhaps that is what I have been taking for granted in my photography that others have seen as something special.

PIERCING BEAUTY
RISHIKESH, INDIA, 2/03

The girl in the photo, "Piercing Beauty," on the preceding page had no idea why I was taking her picture. She has no idea how gorgeous she is or why I even stopped to notice her. She looks at me in wonderment with no fear. She sees me but not herself. I doubt that she will ever know how beautiful she is. So many of my clients are in exactly the same situation. Because of some adverse childhood experiences, they were robbed of the opportunity to experience themselves unencumbered by their shame. They believe they are ugly and do not realize they might be swans and not ducks. In the beginning of treatment, they fight me with all they have in order to maintain their view of themselves as defective. They have very good reasons to do so because they unconsciously fear the consequences of any alternative perspectives. Suffice it to say that, in order to give up their shame, they will have to risk the consequences of giving up their impossible, life-long quest to right a wrong that was never theirs.

INNOCENCE II
RAJAJI NATIONAL PARK, INDIA, 2/03

The lovely girl in the image "Innocence II" on the preceding page lives in a hut in the middle of a jungle that is part of Rajaji National Park in Northern India. How I came to be in the presence of this girl and her family is another one of those fascinatingly wonderfully weird experiences that occurred in India. At the end of February 2003, I was in a city named Haridwar. I went to the Tourist Information Bureau to get a map, and I started talking to a man who worked there. He suggested that I consider going to a hotel that was on the outskirts of this national park. My plan of action in India at this point was to leave my travels to chance. I knew when to catch my departure flight back to the states, and I had a vague idea of the places I wanted to go, but rarely did I stick to an itinerary. I arranged to go to the hotel for a few days. This turned out to be quite a lovely experience because I had an opportunity to ride an elephant in the jungle and also to hire a car to take me on a tour. What I didn't expect was for the man at the Tourist Bureau to show up one evening and announce that the following day he was going to take me to "someplace" in the forest. That someplace turned out to be this young girl's home.

I believe this girl was about nine years old. She was part of a Muslim family that lived in a hut. She had both an older and a younger brother, and their grandfather was also a part of the family unit. This young girl will likely never go to school. She will spend the rest of her life in this jungle. She will be married to some Muslim boy who lives in another hut in the same jungle. The family supports itself by milking some wild animals. I was never able to find out what kind. No one there spoke English, so I was quite fortunate to have my Tourist Bureau guide with me.

I'm sure that I have an overly romantic view of this family. I saw the children playing with the most rudimentary of toys, like a stick they used to hit a ball or a musical instrument that was made by hand from discarded objects. I heard them laughing from a place deep within themselves. They seemed wonderfully content in their lives. When I asked to take the girl's picture, she immediately agreed but asked me to wait for her to change her clothing. The only way she would let me take the shot was if she stood next to her father. You can see the silhouette of her father's head and ear on her right. As I look at her face in this photo, I am reminded of the photograph on page 262, "Islamic Roses," that I took in Cape Town during October 2011.

In this image we see another Muslim girl who was standing in a park. I was attracted to the wonderful contrast between her skin color and what she was wearing. I am now also reminded of the image on page 263, "Afghan Dose." I took this photo in Herat, Afghanistan, during August 1974. This man typified my experience of Afghan men. He was proud, fierce, quite approachable as long as one did so in the correct manner. This image was the first of my photographs that I ever sent out to be seen by a large number of people.

Sometime around 1997, I started to send out a daily email that I called, "the Daily Dose." Initially my doses consisted of one or two quotes that were usually of a spiritual nature. I wanted to share with others a glimpse of the universality of spiritual experience across cultures. The words or forms of this experience might vary, but more often than not, the shared experience is one of inner peace and contentment, and it suggests a connection with something greater. Since then I have sent out a dose every day that I have not been traveling abroad.

During September 2001 it became clear that the United States was getting ready to obliterate much of Afghanistan. I knew from my own experience that before I went to Afghanistan I would not have been able to find it on a map. Because I had such a positive experience in Afghanistan, I wanted to put a face on what we were about to destroy. So for the first time, I included one of my photographs in a dose. That first dose with a picture can be seen on page 263. I certainly did not think of the inclusion of my photography in the doses as any form of art. I was merely trying to show the recipients a part of the world that they most likely would never see on their own. Since then I have sent out more than 3,600 photos. I never send the same photo twice. I've also sent out more than 7,000 quotes for the same reason. Thousands of people all over the world now receive the dose. The dose is free to anyone who would like to receive it.[3] The reactions of the

---

3   http://www.bobshermanphotography.com/subscribe.

recipients to some of my images over the past twelve years have also contributed to my awareness of how my photos have impacted others.

ISLAMIC ROSES
CAPE TOWN, SOUTH AFRICA, 10/11

The above picture is of an Afghan peasant.
It was taken in 1974 in Herat, Afganistan.

"My effort should never be to undermine another's faith but to make him a better follower of his own faith."

Mahatma Gandhi

"Many do not know that we are here in this world to live in harmony. Those who know this do not fight against each other."

Buddhism. The Dhammapada 1:6

The young girls on pages 255 and 257 are both Muslims as is the man pictured on page 263. As I look at these images I see nothing that I would want to kill. During my lifetime, I have seen Germans vilified and then turned into one of our closest allies. The same can be said for the Japanese. In fact, if not for my Japanese-made camera, I probably wouldn't have taken these photos. After that, came the Vietnamese. I could write a separate book about what it was like for me to be in Vietnam in 2007. I was surprised that the Vietnamese did not express anger toward me as an American in their country. I overtly searched for that anger by directly speaking to soldiers who had fought on both sides of the Vietnam War and to people who were either injured themselves or whose children were injured. The universal response to my incredulity about the absence of anger was that it was just not a part of their culture. I have previously written that the hook for me in India was contentment. The hook for me in Vietnam was forgiveness. Even though Iran is currently perceived as one of the more dangerous nations on the planet, when I lived there in 1975 I felt safer there than in many parts of America.

Of course I am aware of events like the terrorist attacks that took place on September 11th. Of course I am aware of people's capacities to justify doing unthinkable crimes to each other. I could probably cite every religion in the world as also being at one time or another responsible for such crimes. I say all of this because the saying, "There but for the grace of God go I," is my absolute truth. I find it impossible to condemn an entire religion, country, or group of people because some of the members of that larger group have committed atrocities. Guilt by association, which leaves no room for individual differences, is unacceptable, and I hope I never fall prey to it. It is also my truth that, more often than not, when I can fully understand how a person got to wherever he or she is, I usually can also understand their actions and motivations.

***

A Moment Of Horror
Shatters Our Illusion Of Control
Sacredly Cherish The Now
And Whatever's In The Fridge

(My holiday card 2001)

CHAPTER THIRTY-ONE
Being a Photographer

When I have a camera around my neck, my field of vision shrinks dramatically. If looking at a landscape, I might for a brief moment take in the entire scene, but very quickly I focus in on the specific source of my attraction. Something happens at that moment that allows me to instantly know what I want to capture. Perhaps a similar process is going on during a therapeutic session. There are countless potential things that I could focus on as my client is talking. Of course, what my client is trying to communicate must be honored, but if listening was all I did, a bartender could replace me. Part of my role is to know what to emphasize and what to ignore, and thereby help my clients see themselves from a different perspective.

I rarely crop my photos when I print them, because I've already imagined the cropping when I framed the shot. The 35mm format renders an image with an aspect ratio of 2:3, and no matter how much you enlarge the original, the resulting image retains that same ratio: 8 x 12, or 12 x 18, or 24 x 36.

However, standard print sizes such as 11 x 14 and 16 x 20 necessitate losing some portion of the image. Instead of perceiving this discrepancy as an interference with my creative process, I use it as a heuristic. In effect, I see the image I want to create within the larger image I have to capture. After years of struggle and practice, I understand now that each photograph I have taken was a tiny, momentary version of my lifelong project to transform my perspective into something that is increasingly more useful. For much of this book, I have been exploring the ways my perspective has changed throughout my life, always resulting in a broader, more comprehensive worldview. Each new experience has allowed me to perceive the world through a wider lens, and thus to see how the limited worldview I had previously imagined as absolute fits into a larger context, just as the picture I ultimately create is contained within the larger image I capture with the photograph. However, it is also possible to get a broader perspective by narrowing the field of view, "To see a world in a grain of sand," as William Blake once wrote. Take for example the following image that I took in a Bangkok temple during February 2011:

Robert Sherman, Ph.D.

ORIGINAL DELICATE

BANGKOK, THAILAND, 2/11

I find this shot to be okay but nothing special. I have others that I took at the same time that I like a lot more. This original photograph is in a 2:3 format. Now let's see what happens when we go into the scene a bit further.

DELICATE - BANGKOK, THAILAND, 2/11

This is the same image cropped and reformatted from portrait to landscape. I prefer the mood this transformation creates; it allows the viewer to move inside this tiny, local world to a more sacred space, which, though smaller, is also greater. Sometimes it *is* better to see the single tree than the entire forest.

Taking a landscape shot requires no courage. There is no risk in shooting a flower. Though, I must admit that, as I write this I am reminded of the time I literally fell off a mountain and found myself tumbling uncontrollably towards a bone-crushing finale. I was fortunate to be wearing a backpack with my tripod strapped to the outside. The tripod saved me when it caught on a small tree. After that I needed my fourth knee surgery, and I had a torn rotator cuff in my left shoulder. I didn't even get any decent shots!

Most of the time when taking a portrait I find I don't have to muster a lot of courage either. Rarely has someone objected when I've asked to take his or her picture. Of course, I try to respect the cultural norms wherever I am. For example, in most Islamic cultures it's not okay to take a woman's picture. I can only think of one time in which I was almost too intimidated to take any shots. I was in Costa Rica, and I saw a group of people who attracted me. As I walked towards them, I felt a sense of intimidation. I did not know how they might react to a *gringo* wanting to take their picture. Perhaps it was the language barrier. I finally created an opening by taking a picture of a child and then showing his mother the image on the camera's LCD screen.

Others gathered around, and I took more pictures. As I started to show them the shots, more people became amenable. What had started off as an uneasy and tentative experience turned into a lot of fun. I later learned that the reason they had been standing there was that they were all waiting for a truck to pick them up. This truck functioned as their bus to take them home.

I took the picture on page 275, "I Know," at that time. I love how the color and texture of the subject's face is almost the same as the wall he is leaning against. I'm attracted to how relaxed he is at that moment. We had all collaborated through patience and communication to create the atmosphere of safety that resulted in this photograph.

The rules of the game of therapy allow me to feel a similar sense of safety during the therapeutic process. My childhood experience rendered me sensitive to my own fear of engulfment. This fear still sometimes inhibits my ability to be fully open to people outside of my office. Over the years, I have learned how to participate in the therapeutic process with clear boundaries that I am confident of being able to assert and maintain. Possibly the boundary my camera creates allows me to feel safe enough to get closer to a stranger than I would otherwise do. I know that part of my growth involves learning to expand my capacity to feel safe. I have learned that from that safe place my capacity for love and compassion flows with ease. Intellectually, I understand that these limitations lie within myself and not the external situation.

My impression before I went to Cambodia in 2007 was that it would not be okay for me to talk to the monks or take pictures of them. So the first day that I was at Angkor Wat, I spent twenty minutes on a photographic safari, stalking two young monks who were walking and talking to each other. After twenty minutes, I decided that this pursuit was not at all to my liking, so I approached one of them.

"May I take your picture," I asked.

"Do you speak English?" he asked.

"Yes," I said.

"Do you mind if I speak English?"

"Please do."

He had such a childlike laugh.

"I've never spoken English to anyone before," he said.

He had studied English by listening to the radio. We spent about thirty minutes engaged in a most lovely conversation. I took the picture on page 276, "Contemplation," as he walked away after we had concluded our interaction. Angkor Wat is a massive area and is home to many Buddhist temples. For me, this shot captures the contemplative nature of the monk's monastic existence.

Vietnam was a delightful surprise. The people were warm and eager to make contact. The food was spectacular. Much of the scenery was breathtaking. I took the picture on page 277, "Other Worldly," in Ha Long Bay, which is located in the northeast corner of Vietnam. My son Jonas and I spent three great days on a boat similar to the one in the image. The looming Karst Mountains transform the bay into an alien landscape. The framing of this shot was by no means an accident. I chose to frame the boat in the spotlight on the water in order to suggest an otherworldly feeling to the entire scene. That is also why I rendered the colors the way I did.

I KNOW
CARRIZAL, COSTA RICA, 12/09

Robert Sherman, Ph.D.

CONTEMPLATION
ANGKOR WAT, CAMBODIA, 11/07

OTHER WORLDLY - HA LONG BAY, VIETNAM, 11/07

I took the photograph on the following page, "Ghost in the Alley," in Varanasi, India, during March 2003. It is a four-minute time exposure taken at about 3:30 a.m. If you look carefully, you will see the outline of a man at the end of the alley. This is "the ghost" in the shot. In reality it is a man wheeling a bicycle. When he entered the alleyway, he saw my tripod and me and stopped. I asked him to just remain still because I knew this shot was almost complete. Because of the low light in the alleyway and because he remained in the shot for only twenty seconds, the camera captured his faint outline as a ghost. The blue cast in the light is the true color of shade, not something that I added. During the day I would not have paid any attention to such a scene, but the darkness created a mood that allowed me to see this alley in a very different way. There is actually a fair amount of garbage in the photo. This is one of my favorite images.

GHOST IN THE ALLEY

VARANASI, INDIA, 3/03

My faith and understanding allow me the realization that very often I do not have enough information to be able to fully understand or control what is happening. I illustrate this to my clients by holding a piece of paper up against their faces so close that they are unable see what it is or what is written on it. I then ask them to tell me what I'm holding. It is not illiteracy that prevents them from being able to discern what is printed on the paper; it is merely a matter of perspective. As soon as they are far enough away, they have no difficulty reading what is so clearly there. As part of my spiritual practice, I try to maintain this awareness that, most of the time, I am too close to a situation to fully appreciate how it fits into the whole.

I know that when I am thoroughly immersed in my passion for the next shot I want to take, I never have anyone else in mind. I know that, at that moment, I am only trying to please myself. This is the exact opposite of what takes place during psychotherapy. In the therapeutic process, I am focused exclusively on my clients' experience of their existence. But both endeavors lead to the same place. Both endeavors seek to reveal a deeper truth, because I do believe that in the revelation of that truth we have the opportunity to be set free.

CHAPTER THIRTY-TWO
A Recent Lesson

I wrote the first draft of this book between January and June 2012. On November 6, 2012, I had both of my knees replaced. Prior to the surgery, my surgeon had told me that he would not schedule me for a follow up appointment until at least six weeks post op. His assistant told me the surgeon knew if I saw him prior to that time, I would be in so much pain that I would want to kill him. After six weeks he'd be glad to see me because I would be feeling so much better than I had prior to the surgery. As a result of this information, I anticipated six weeks of hell, especially since I was having both knees done at the same time. Then I could move on with my life.

The day after my surgery, two physical therapists came into my room and asked me to walk from my bed to the door. I asked them if I would hurt myself if I kept walking to the nurses' station. They looked at each other like they thought I was delusional, but they assured me my restraints would protect me.

"If you think you can do it," one of them added, "then go for it."

So we walked to the nurses' station. I will not bore you with the next eleven months of physical therapy except for a few more things. I approached my recovery by always doing more than suggested— as long as I wasn't putting myself in danger. By the seventeenth day after my surgery, I gave up my walker. And on the nineteenth day, I was driving myself to physical therapy. To be truthful, the driving was the only part that I did against medical advice. I had fun with a rehab nurse who I asked to explain the prohibition against driving.

"You will not be able to react quickly enough or be able to withstand the pressure of your foot on the brake," she said.

As she was telling me this, I deliberately stepped on her foot and increased the pressure until finally she started to laugh. It was clear that I could apply far more pressure than I'd need for a brake pedal.

During the eighth week, I met with my surgeon. He took X-rays and was very happy with his work. I showed him that both legs had a range of motion that I shouldn't have expected for a year. There was only one fly in my ointment. The movement still caused me a great deal of pain.

"Sometimes that happens," my doctor said.

"What do you have that will help?" I asked.

"Want to go to a pain clinic?"

It took a great deal of restraint on my part to not give in to my impulse to cause him an equal amount of pain so that he could go to his pain clinic for me. I had not gone through the surgery and physical therapy in order to learn how to adapt to more pain than I'd had prior to the replacements. Left to my own devices, I went back to my physical therapy.

About a week later, my physical therapist instructed me to try a new exercise. I had to lie on my stomach with a band tied around an ankle. As I pulled on the band, it forced my leg to bend. This exercise was extraordinarily painful, but I persisted through the pain. When I was done, I felt totally spent and sort of like a zombie. At the start of my next physical therapy session, I was about to tell the therapist that I'd like to pass on that exercise. But before I could say a word, she told me that we weren't going to do that one again. Clearly she saw something.

For the next nine months, I experienced a great deal of pain much of the time and that unusual zombie state at least once per week. I also started seeing a masterful massage therapist named Janice Cathey. Many of my sessions with her were also quite painful. During one of them, she was working on my right leg, and I began to feel a great deal of pain but also a tremendous amount of sadness. Somehow I instinctively knew that this sadness was not coming from my surgery. She was tapping into stored emotional remnants from my abusive childhood. I pleaded with her to trust that I was capable knowing my own limits, and I asked her not to stop regardless of my tears. Out of her skill, faith, and love, she was able to accompany me on the journeys that followed. What became clear to me was that much of my knee pain all of my adult life had resulted as much from stored emotion as from bad knee genes and bowed legs. But I was only able to see Janice once per month, so I saw another massage therapist who I jokingly referred to as the "truck driver" because my body felt like it was being run over by a truck during and after our sessions. To be clear, she did a great job of doing exactly what I asked her to do.

I continued physical therapy and massage therapy for eleven and a half months. My pain gradually began to dissipate. After about nine months, I was finally back to my pre-surgical level of pain, and that's as good as it got.

"I'd like for you to consider that pushing your body through this much pain really isn't very kind or loving," Janice said during one of our sessions.

"That may be true, but that's the way I have been living all of my life. I never could have survived my childhood or gotten my Ph.D. if I had done it any other way."

"Well your body may be rebelling against all the pain and pressure."

Janice's words stayed with me. I started to really take a look at those times that I had to zone out to endure the pain and how I felt after those sessions. A while later, I was at a memorial service for a recently deceased friend. As the service progressed I found myself writing the following poem.

Time to Love the Pain Away

A sudden realization
After 67 years of pain
What looked like strength and endurance
Was really perseverance through the remnants of my
shame

My body kept on dialing
But I never answered the phone
How sad to be an outsider
In the middle of my own home

Time to say yes to life and love
To stop pushing against the tide
Time to allow for the reality
Of the joy that's trapped inside

I will now ease my pain away
And trust the safety of love
I will stop the pushing
And welcome the abundance
That rains down from above

I now believe that those zombie-like states were remnants of what I had to do to survive my sexual abuse experiences. If I continue to willingly inflict huge amounts of pain as part of my rehabilitation, I will continue to re-traumatize myself. It is now my intention to stop my physical therapy and to substitute taking walks in nature and to get back into regular yoga practices. It's time for me to stop the endurance race that has characterized much of my existence.

CHAPTER THIRTY-THREE
Where Do I Go From Here?

So three hundred pages later I'm still a Hinjew shrink photographer in Brentwood, Tennessee. I've taken you on a journey around my external and internal worlds. I'm sixty-eight years old, and I am definitely on the other side of the slope. Of course, I have no idea how long the slope is. I am fortunate in that, despite having a bunch of miles on my tires, my chassis is holding up fairly well. There is still an abundance of places that I would love to experience and photograph. I still eagerly await my next opportunity to get on a motorcycle in some third-world country to arrive at some unknown destination in order to play and take pictures.

I have asked my sons to carefully think about what they want from me that I have not yet given or shared with them. I was delightfully surprised and deeply touched when, independently, each of them told me that they would like for us to go on another trip to India together. I'm not sure that their lives will allow for this to take place. Many years ago before we did go to India together (in 2005), I wrote into my will that I wanted to be cremated with a cheese danish and have my sons throw my ashes into the Ganges River in Varanasi. This will be my way of honoring my "Hinjew roots." But more importantly, it is my way of trying to ensure that each of them will have an opportunity to experience a place that has been so significant in my life. It would be truly wonderful if we do get the chance to go back there together again with me not in a box.

In the preceding pages, I have attempted to share with you some of the central themes in the story of my life. I have given you a glimpse into the roots of my shame and my subsequent journey towards the truth. I have attempted to share the significant influences that have shaped my perspective on who I am and what my life is all about. I tell my clients that I do not have an altruistic molecule in my body. I tell them that everything that I do, I try to do in whatever way will allow me to like what I see when I look in the mirror. These days when I look in the mirror, I see a definite need for liposuction and perhaps a few other minor procedures. I'm still very much a work in progress. I have much to learn about forgiveness and contentment. I still have much to learn about how to continue to improve my vision so that I can see the inherent beauty in everything. I still have a long way to go to fully get past my fears of engulfment. Intellectually, I firmly believe that it is possible to get to a place in which I am so firmly rooted in the direct experience of abundance that the notion of being sucked dry would be both inconceivable and ridiculous.

As I write this now, I am sitting in my office, not the place where I practice professionally, but the room in our home where I process my photographs and send out the "Daily Dose."

I have now been in a relationship with my exquisitely beautiful wife, Beth, for sixteen years. We finally got married at the start of 2011. There are times when our relationship is so frustrating for each of us that it appears that the Arabs and the Israelis will sign a peace accord long before we can reach a successful resolution of our differences. So far, we have managed to reach the depths of our despair, and from that place we have found a way to persevere. This perseverance is not a process of martyrdom—though sometimes it does feel that way. It is truly the fire that has potential to purify. It allows me to see the echoes of my parents' negative influences and my own baggage that even liposuction can't remove. And isn't it just so wonderful that I serve the same purpose for her? (I told you that marriages were made in heaven). But this is certainly not all that we have. Each of us gives the other the opportunity to see the world through vastly different eyes, and we certainly attempt to communicate in very different ways. It's obvious to me that in order for relationships to truly allow for the fullest manifestation of each member's potential, the vastly different ways that men and women are in the world need to be honored as equally valid. My wife's chaotically creative way of being causes me to flip switches and blow fuses that I didn't even know I had. And, it offers me yet another wonderful way to push past the shame and fear that have stunted aspects of my creativity. She doesn't suffer from the same social awkwardness that I do, and so, as I tag along on her journey, I get to meet some wonderful people who otherwise would have never crossed my path. In addition, she has these exquisite lips that she frequently uses to produce either music that touches people's souls or kisses that touch mine. Each of us offers the other a marvelous opportunity to feel and expand our capacities to love, to feel loved, and to experience the divine.

Nevertheless I'm still writing this from Brentwood, Tennessee. Sadly I'm beginning to realize that Brentwood is really only an acute example of an underlying condition that may be permeating much of Western society and that my adverse experiences with local politics and religious limitations are not unique to the deep South. During the last four years, we have witnessed the Arab Spring, in which previously mistreated people have risen up to risk their lives for something better. It remains to be seen what will ultimately come from their efforts. Meanwhile, the people of America appear to have entered into some form of semi-comatose state in which they are either incapable or unwilling to do the same for themselves. A year ago a congressional committee made up entirely of men testified about women's reproductive rights. All that was missing from their expertise was a graphic demonstration of their capacities for childbearing and breast-feeding. During April 2012, the Holy See censured the Leadership Conference of Women

Religious, an organization that represents eighty percent of the nuns in America, because they were spending too much of their time and resources on helping the poor and not enough time enforcing the church's teachings against homosexuality, abortion and same-sex marriage. Now there is a wonderfully different Pope who has said some remarkably loving and inclusive things. It remains to be seen whether his words will be translated into significant actions.

The years from the Reagan Administration in the 1980s to now have been characterized by a vast redistribution of wealth in America. As the pay of CEOs goes up, the standard of living of the middle and lower classes in America goes down. The attacks on the rights of working people have become flagrant, and yet there are no significant mass protests. The brokers and bankers continue to flaunt their greed. While millions of people have lost their homes and significant wealth, these bankers and brokers have seen their net worth increase without any significant public protest.

In 1963 when my father told me that my college education was up to me, I was able to attend the City University of New York at a cost that I was able to afford. The quality of that education was superb. By the time I completed my doctorate, I believe that I had no more than $10,000 in outstanding loans. I was able to make enough money to easily pay off those student loans in a timely manner. There is no way that the students of today will be able to pay off the trillion dollars of outstanding student loans, and yet there's no significant public outcry. A couple of days ago, a British friend of mine was describing what's going on in England now. What he described is exactly the same process that I am outlining here. I do not have the expertise to know whether or not a similar process is going on in many other Western countries.

In 1974, I went off to India on a spiritual quest. Somehow in the midst of all of that material poverty, I was blessed to be able to find what I was looking for. It would not at all surprise me if during my sons' lifetimes it will be the Indians who will be coming to America in search of their own spiritual experience. In the universe, when a star is getting ready to die, it does not go out with a whimper. Instead it puffs itself up and burns brighter than ever before it's gone. Perhaps that is what we see happening now with some aspects of organized religion and our Western domination of the world. The number of middle-class Indians now exceeds the total population of America. Very soon the Chinese economy will surpass America's. When I first started traveling to third-world countries, it was staggering to see the vast discrepancy between the very rich and the very poor. It seems to me that the same thing is happening here now. Of course, I have no idea how these events will unfold.

During 2007, I had the good fortune to spend some time with a man who won a Nobel Peace prize. This man has done some truly wonderful things during his lifetime. He was able to bring about fantastic change in his country. He was able to see possibilities when so many others could not. So I pleaded with him to allow me to see America through his eyes. I asked him if he saw any signs that would give him reason for optimism. Sadly he told me that he did not see any. During the same conversation, I spoke to him about my hope that the world of Islam would see the rise of its own Gandhi or Martin Luther King Junior. Today I have the same hope and prayer that very soon the political landscape in America will see the rise of a very different leader who will seek to encourage the best in us rather than to control us through fear and ignorance.

The Hindus believe that eventually the universe will be sucked back into its primordial form to then spend time waiting for it to again be recreated. They also believe that who we really are is our spirit, which is immortal. So in reality, the economic and social conditions that I am describing will not affect whomever we really are. And, since the universe exists in order to provide us with the experiences we need to foster our spiritual growth, all of this is exactly as it should be. But that part of me that is still a work in progress believes it may be close to the time when Shiva should hit the reset button. So the truth is, I really have no idea at all what is now growing in my Brentwood Petri dish.

I've enjoyed writing this book. I know that my current clients are a wonderful group of people to work with. I am currently seeing a number of people between the ages of twenty-three and thirty-three. They are blowing me away with their strong desire for growth and their ability to do the work. I am also seeing many people whose childhood religious experiences have greatly exacerbated their shame. They too bring a hunger for something different to their process.

I hope that one day I will have an opportunity for a gallery show of my photography. Perhaps my show will be the shots that I have shared with you in this book.

I often suggest to my clients that they think about lying on their deathbeds. I then encourage them to watch the final movie of their existence—their last chance for the final grades of their lives. I tell them that they have a choice between two movies. After watching one of the choices, they will be filled with regrets. After watching the other movie, they will notice some tears coming down the sides of their faces and they will hear themselves saying, "Wow…What a hell of a ride! Bye." Pick one.

***

The Illusion Of An Infinite Amount Of Time
Swept Away By The Reminders Of Age
Say It And Do It Now
So That Gratitude And Not Regret Prevails.

(My holiday card 2002)